MAYDAYS

Edgar's epic play of political life since 1945 received enormous critical acclaim when premiered at the Barbican Theatre in 1983. Originally published to coincide with that production, the play is now reissued in a completely reset, definitive, post-production edition.

'Dazzling new offering . . . A looking-glass to our time, this is surely one of the most important plays of the decade, certainly one of the most courageous and stimulating.'　*City Limits*

'David Edgar's magnificent new play for the Royal Shakespeare Company is an epic, brilliantly plotted piece of writing that takes revolution as its theme and the particular fate of three characters as its subject . . . More successful than any other recent British play, *Maydays* wrestles with the undeniable fact that liberty to say what you like is not quite the same thing as political liberation.'　*Financial Times*

Front cover design by The Drawing Room, Warwick.
The photograph of David Edgar on the back cover is by
Chris Davies.

by the same author

WRECKERS (Eyre Methuen, 1977)
DESTINY (Eyre Methuen, 1978)
DICK DETERRED (Monthly Review Press, New York, 1974)
TWO KINDS OF ANGEL
   (in *The London Fringe Theatre*, Burnham House, 1975)
THE JAIL DIARY OF ALBIE SACHS (Rex Collings, 1978)
BALL BOYS (Pluto Press, 1978)
TEENDREAMS (Eyre Methuen, 1979)
MARY BARNES (Eyre Methuen, 1979)

David Edgar

MAYDAYS

METHUEN · LONDON AND NEW YORK

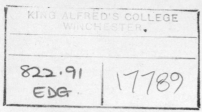
A METHUEN PAPERBACK

First published as a Methuen paperback original in 1983
by Methuen London Ltd, 11 New Fetter Lane, London
EC4P 4EE
Re-issued in this reset, revised and definitive edition in 1984
Copyright © 1983, 1984 by David Edgar
Set in IBM 10 point Journal by ⩔ Tek-Art, Croydon, Surrey
Printed in Great Britain by
Richard Clay (The Chaucer Press) Ltd,
Bungay, Suffolk

British Library Cataloguing in Publication Data

Edgar, David
    Maydays. — 2nd ed. — (Methuen modern plays)
    I. Title
    822'.914   PR6055.D44
    ISBN 0-413-57080-0

Maydays

To Jill Forbes

1956

February   Krushchev condemns Stalin at Twentieth Party Congress

June   Polish strikes put down by government troops

October   British troops invade Suez

November   Soviet troops invade Hungary

1958

February   Campaign for Nuclear Disarmament (CND) founded

1959

February   Castro takes power in Cuba

1960

March   Sharpeville massacre in South Africa

1961

August   Berlin Wall constructed

September   Mass arrests in Trafalgar Square during anti-nuclear sit-down

1962

October   Cuban missile crisis

1963

November   President Kennedy assassinated

1964

August   Three civil rights workers murdered in Mississippi; 'Gulf of Tonkin' Incident led to escalation of war in Vietnam

October   Krushchev falls from power

1965

November   Pentagon immobilised by anti-war protestors

1966

February   Russian dissident writers Sinyavsky and Daniel sentenced to labour camps for publishing their writings in the West

1967

January	Dissidents demonstrate in Pushkin Square, Moscow, against tightening of Soviet Criminal Code
July	Black riots in Detroit and Newark
October	Che Guevara killed in Bolivia

1968

January	Viet Cong threaten Saigon in Tet offensive
March	Mass demonstration at American Embassy in Grosvenor Square
	Lyndon Johnson withdraws from Presidential race
April	Martin Luther King assassinated
	Enoch Powell delivers speech against black immigration
May	Students' and workers' uprising in France
June	Robert Kennedy assassinated
August	Riots during Democratic convention at Chicago; Soviet troops invade Czechoslovakia
November	President Nixon elected

1969

July	500,000 attend rock festival at Woodstock, N.Y.
August	British troops sent into Northern Ireland

1970

March	Three underground anti-war protestors blown up by own bomb in New York
April	American troops invade Cambodia
May	During protest demonstrations six students killed by National Guard at Jackson State and Kent State Universities
June	Successful mass campaign against South African cricket tour to Great Britain
	Jewish Soviet dissidents hijack airplane in Leningrad
	Edward Heath elected Prime Minister
September	Salvador Allende elected President of Chile
December	Strikes in Poland lead to resignation of Communist leader

1971

January	'Angry Brigade' bombs home of Employment Minister in protest against Industrial Relations Act
June	Upper Clyde shipbuilders' 'work-in' begins
August	Internment without trial begins in Northern Ireland

1972

January	Miners' strike leads to electricity black-outs; 'Bloody Sunday' massacre in Londonderry, Northern Ireland
February	Miners win seven-week strike
March	Direct rule imposed in Northern Ireland
June	Break-in at Democratic headquarters in Watergate; Five dockers jailed at Pentonville for defying Industrial Relations Act: released after Trades Unions protest
September	Eleven Israeli athletes killed by pro-Palestinian guerillas at Munich Olympics
December	Four members of 'Angry Brigade' sentenced

1973

March	IRA bombs the Old Bailey
May	2,000,000 workers in Britain on May Day strike
September	Allende overthrown by military coup in Chile
December	State of Emergency declared in second Miners' dispute; Three Day Week imposed

1974

February	Edward Heath calls General Election; Wilson elected
	Solzhenitsyn expelled from USSR
April	Fascism overthrown in Portugal
July	Military rule ends in Greece
August	President Nixon resigns over Watergate cover-up

1975

February	Margaret Thatcher defeats Edward Heath to become Conservative Party leader
April	Communist victory in Cambodia and Vietnam
May	Baader-Meinhof terrorist trial begins in Stuttgart

	Britain votes 'yes' in EEC referendum
July	Wilson imposes £6 income policy
November	Franco dies in Spain
	Revolutionary government takes over in Angola

1976

March	Wilson resigns; Callaghan elected Labour Party leader
June	Soweto killings in South Africa
August	Notting Hill Carnival Riots
September	Chairman Mao dies
October	'Gang of Four' arrested

1977

January	Czech dissidents publish Charter 77
June	Mass pickets in Grunwick unionisation dispute
September	Steve Biko dies in detention in South Africa

1978

March	Aldo Moro, former Italian Prime Minister kidnapped and killed by Red Brigades
April	Anti-Nazi carnival in London
July	Soviet dissidents Ginzberg and Shcharansky sentenced to long terms in labour camps
December	Vietnamese troops invade Kampuchea

1979

January	Wave of public service strikes dubbed 'Winter of Discontent'
February	Shah deposed in Iranian revolution
April	Nuclear crisis at Three Mile Island power plant in Pennsylvania
	Blair Peach dies in Southall anti-National Front demonstration
May	Margaret Thatcher elected Prime Minister
November	American embassy hostages seized in Iran; Conservative government decides to deploy Cruise missiles in Great Britain
December	USSR invades Afghanistan

1980

August Gdansk shipyard strikes lead to founding of independent trade union 'Solidarity' in Poland

November Ronald Reagan elected President of USA

1981

February Social Democratic Party formed in Great Britain

May 'H' Block hunger strikes by IRA prisoners in Maze prison

July Riots in Toxteth, Brixton and Moss Side

September Labour Party votes for unilateral disarmament; Women's Peace Camp first set up at Greenham Common

December Martial law imposed in Poland

Maydays was first presented by the Royal Shakespeare Company at the Barbican Theatre, London, on 13 October 1983, with the following cast:

JEREMY CROWTHER	John Shrapnel
PAVEL LERMONTOV	Bob Peck
MIKLOS PALOCZI	Ken Bones
CLARA IVANOVNA	Stephanie Fayerman
OLD WOMAN	Brenda Peters
FORGACH	Raymond Bowers
SOVIET SOLDIERS	Richard Clifford, William Haden, Robert Clare, Robin Meredith, John Tramper
HUNGARIAN PRISONERS	Simon Clark, Floyd Bevan, Alexandra Brook
MARTIN GLASS	Antony Sher
CLARK SULLIVAN	David Troughton
CATHY WEINER	Lesley Sharp
JAMES GRAIN	Malcolm Storry
AMANDA	Alison Steadman
PHIL MANDRELL	Brian Parr
BRIAN	Phillip Walsh
JUDY	Sara Mair-Thomas
PUGACHEV	Geoffrey Freshwater
STUDENT	Floyd Bevan
POLICEMAN	Raymond Bowers
TEDDY WEINER	Don Fellows
OFFICIAL (MVD)	Robin Meredith
DETECTIVE	Geoffrey Freshwater
KOROLENKO	David Troughton
PRISONER	Simon Clark
OFFICER	William Haden
DOCTOR	Anna Fox
CHIEF OFFICER	Robin Meredith

PAPERSELLERS	William Haden, Richard Clifford, Simon Clark, Floyd Bevan, Anna Fox, John Tramper
RON	Robert Clare
LIBERTARIANS	Floyd Bevan, Alexandra Brook, Lesley Sharp
MRS GLASS	Brenda Peters
SMOKING PARTYGOER	William Haden
MOLLY	Stephanie Fayerman
OFFICIAL (FRANKFURT)	Raymond Bowers
YOUNG MAN	Brian Parr
HUGH TRELAWNEY	Tony Church
TANIA	Jayne Tottman
WOMEN	Anna Fox, Alexandra Brook, Lesley Sharp

Directed by Ron Daniels
Set designed by John Gunter
Costumes designed by Di Seymour
Music by Stephen Oliver
Lighting by Chris Ellis
Sound by John Leonard

The play takes places in England, Hungary, the United States and the Soviet Union. It begins in 1945 and ends in the early 1980s.

The play was written to use doubling extensively. It may be performed comfortably by a company of 14 men and 5 women.

Act One

It has always been an intellectual axiom that Britain is half-dead, and if there is no rallying-point abroad, some people are going to do no rallying at all. It would not occur to them that the Welfare State is worth rallying to. At home, indeed, very few causes offer themselves to the cruising rebel. No more millions out of work, no more hunger-marches, no more strikes; none at least that the rebel can take an interest in, when the strike pay-packet is likely to be as much as he gets himself for a review of Evelyn Waugh or a talk about basset-horns on the Third Programme . . .

Kingsley Amis, *Socialism and the Intellectuals,* **1956**

A number of Western commentators have stressed the role of a 'generation gap' in the rise of Soviet dissent. According to this theory, dissent is largely the work of the post-war generation. This younger generation was shocked and repelled by the revelations of its parents' complicity, whether active or passive, in Stalin's repressions; having grown up in relative security and prosperity, it is more willing to assume the risks of outspoken criticism than its elders, who cherish the peace and stability they have at last achieved. From this perspective, Soviet dissent may appear to be a local branch of the world-wide youth rebellion of the late sixties and early seventies, rejecting, like its foreign counterparts, 'bourgeois' materialism, social conformity and political hypocrisy . . .

Marshall S Shatz, *Soviet Dissent: Historical Perspectives,* **1969**

In the advanced capitalist countries, the radicalization of the working class is counteracted by a socially-engineered arrest of consciousness, and by the development and satisfaction of needs which perpetuate the servitude of the exploited . . . No economic or political changes will bring this historical continuum to a stop unless they are carried through by men who are physiologically able to experience things, and each other, outside the context of violence and exploitation.

Herbert Marcuse, *An Essay on Liberation,* **1969**

ACT ONE

Scene One

May Day, 1945. England.

Red flags fly, red banners swirl, red streamers billow. 'The Internationale' plays.

Through the hangings marches a young man, JEREMY CROWTHER, *at the age of 17. In his northern voice, nervously at first, but growing in strength, he addresses a large, enthusiastic — even triumphant — crowd.*

JEREMY CROWTHER. Comrades. This May Day of all May Days it is a privilege to deliver the fraternal greetings of the Young Communist League.

Comrades, it was the great V.I. Lenin who once said, revolutions are festivals of the oppressed and the exploited. Today of all days, the working-class has cause for festive celebration. The Great Anti-Fascist war is won. All over Europe, warmongers and capitalists are shaking in their shoes.

Comrades, we have been asked a thousand times what we mean by socialism. As throughout the continent the toiling masses rise to liberate themselves from tyranny, to fashion with their own hands their own New Jerusalem, we can at last say: *this* is what we meant.

'The Internationale' cuts out. The hangings fly away.

Scene Two

A military barracks in Budapest, 5 November 1956. Upstage, a bench, one Soviet SOLDIER *by the exit, a* 2ND SOLDIER *and a* SERGEANT *by the bench. A Hungarian civilian* PRISONER *sitting on the bench, hands on head. In addition to the scripted events in the upstage area, there is a constant bustle going on, busy people marching to and fro with papers and documents. Downstage, a little office area, with a table and three chairs, on one of which a Soviet Army* STENOGRAPHER *sits typing. On her table are a pile of files, a cardboard box, and a radio, from which an operetta tune is emanating. Two* PRISONERS *are marched in by a* 3RD SOLDIER.

3RD SOLDIER. At the double move move move.

SERGEANT. Name.

2ND PRISONER. Szilagyi, Bela.

SERGEANT. Name.

The 3RD PRISONER *does not reply.*

Name!

3RD PRISONER. Paloczi, Miklos.

SERGEANT. Sit. Hands on head.

They do so, as a Soviet lieutenant, PAVEL LERMONTOV, *comes into the office, from a side entrance. He is twenty-seven. The* STENOGRAPHER *stands quickly; after a moment, she switches off the radio.*

LERMONTOV. You like operetta, comrade?

STENOGRAPHER (*after a second*). Oh yes, comrade lieutenant, very much. Do you?

LERMONTOV. Well, yes, yes.

He looks in the cardboard box. It is full of the paraphernalia of urban guerilla war: broken milk bottles, oily rags, a piece of chain, a flick-knife, a hammer, a couple of hand-grenades. As he does so, a 4TH SOLDIER *marches a* 4TH PRISONER *into the upstage area, and the* 2ND SOLDIER *brings files into the office, puts them on the desk, and goes upstage.*

SERGEANT. Name.

4TH PRISONER. Erica Molnar.

SERGEANT. Molnar, Erica. Sit down.

She sits down as the STENOGRAPHER *reaches out to put the radio on.*

LERMONTOV. But perhaps, not now.

He picks up a file and looks through it.

STENOGRAPHER. It's a very beautiful city. Perhaps that's why they produce such beautiful music.

LERMONTOV. Yes, I think, in fact . . . Where do you come from, comrade?

STENOGRAPHER. Oh, just a small village, Comrade Lermontov.

LERMONTOV. And have you ever been to Moscow? Leningrad?

The STENOGRAPHER *shakes her head, smiling. A* 5TH PRISONER *is brought in by the* 3RD SOLDIER, *who shakes his head at the* SERGEANT.

Well, they are beautiful cities, too. And they have their music.

He's making to go upstage, as the 5TH PRISONER *sits. A thought strikes him.*

What's your name?

STENOGRAPHER. Clara Ivanovna.

LERMONTOV. No, I meant — no, that will do. Clara Ivanovna, summon for me, if you will, M. Paloczi.

The STENOGRAPHER *goes to the upper area and calls.*

STENOGRAPHER. M. Paloczi!

The SERGEANT *nods to the* 3RD PRISONER. *The* 2ND *and* 3RD SOLDIERS *pull him to his feet and push him into the office. He is* MIKLOS PALOCZI, *twenty-one years old, wearing a long grey overcoat and a slouch hat. He looks a bit like a gangster. His face is bruised and there are traces of blood. The* STENOGRAPHER *comes back to her table. The* SERGEANT *goes out.*

LERMONTOV. Sit.

> PALOCZI *sits. The* SOLDIERS *withdraw. The*
> STENOGRAPHER *picks up a notepad and pencil.*
> LERMONTOV *is consulting the file as he speaks.*

My name is Lt Lermontov. Your name is Miklos Paloczi. You
are twenty-one years old, and a student. You were arrested at
three o'clock this morning, in charge of a radio transmitter
broadcasting illegally from a lodging in the Corvin Alley
district.

PALOCZI *says nothing.*

Yesterday afternoon, you made a broadcast of an apparently
slanderous character. Your broadcast was as follows:

He reads:

'Comrades, take care! Counter-revolutionaries are everywhere.
No less than ten million landowners and capitalists and —
bishops roam the country, laying waste to all that they
survey. Even the strongholds of the proletariat have not
escaped infection. Forty thousand aristocrats and fascists are
on strike in Csepel, aided and abetted by the forces of
imperialism. Comrades, vigilance! The revolution is in danger.'
    Could you explain this to me, please?

PALOCZI *says nothing.*

I'm afraid I don't speak Hungarian. Do you speak Russian?

Slight pause.

I speak German just a little.

Slight pause.

English?

PALOCZI. I can speak Russian. We can all speak Russian.

LERMONTOV. Good.

PALOCZI. 'Csepel' is pronounced 'Shaypell'. It is a large
  industrial district to the south of Budapest. It's where a
  general strike is going on. You may have heard about it.
  Budapest is the city you have just invaded. It is the capital of

Hungary, an independent Republic of ten million people —

LERMONTOV. You're saying that the working-class of — Csepel, are all fascists?

Pause. PALOCZI *shakes his head.*

PALOCZI. I was being — irony. Ironical.

LERMONTOV. Comrade, I would seriously advise you not to be too clever. It was, after all, your government who invited us to aid you, in your struggle against the White Terror and reaction.

There is a commotion developing upstage. An OLD WOMAN, *dressed in black, and carrying a string bag, is forcing her way in from the street, past the* 1ST SOLDIER.

OLD WOMAN. Where are my sausages?

1ST SOLDIER. Hey, you can't go in there —

LERMONTOV. We are all well aware of where we are, and why we're here.

OLD WOMAN (*to a* 2ND SOLDIER). Hey, you! I want my sausages.

LERMONTOV *aware of the commotion.*

2ND SOLDIER. What's this?

1ST SOLDIER. I don't know, it's some old —

LERMONTOV (*to* PALOCZI). Please excuse me.

LERMONTOV *and the* STENOGRAPHER *to the doorway between the office and the upstage area.*

2ND SOLDIER (*taking the* OLD WOMAN'*s arm*). Now, granny, you can't come in here.

1ST SOLDIER. She's crazy.

OLD WOMAN. Come on, where are they? Hey?

LERMONTOV (*to the* STENOGRAPHER). Find out what's going on.

STENOGRAPHER. She wants something I think.

LERMONTOV. That much is clear. Please find out what, and why.

The STENOGRAPHER *to upstage area.*

OLD WOMAN. You said that there'd be sausages on Monday. And some beetroot. I demand my sausages!

She breaks free.

PALOCZI. I can tell you what she wants.

STENOGRAPHER (*to* 1ST SOLDIER). What's going on?

1ST SOLDIER. Oh, some old crazy Magyar thinks we're s'posed to feed her.

The OLD WOMAN *is trying to find her sausages. The first* TWO SOLDIERS *in chase. The* 3RD SOLDIER *nervously keeping the* PRISONERS *covered.*

OLD WOMAN. Where are you hiding them?

1ST SOLDIER. Now, come on, granny, off we go —

PALOCZI (*to* LERMONTOV). Till yesterday, this barracks was a distribution centre. For the free food that the peasants brought us from the villages.

2ND SOLDIER (*grabbing the* OLD WOMAN). There — is — no — food. Here — is — the — army. There — is — no — entry — here.

The OLD WOMAN *is at the exit.*

OLD WOMAN. Huh. All the same. You take the food and fuck the peasants, eh? This time, 'the real revolution'?

The FEMALE PRISONER *laughs. The* 3RD SOLDIER *threatens her. The* OLD WOMAN *spits.*

Tchah. Budapesti.

The 1ST SOLDIER *manhandles her out.* LERMONTOV *suddenly, to* PALOCZI:

LERMONTOV. Free food?

PALOCZI. That's right.

LERMONTOV. The peasants bring the cities food, for nothing?

PALOCZI. You know, it's no wonder you're all told to stay inside your tanks. Or else you might find out what's happening here.

The STENOGRAPHER *returning.*

LERMONTOV. So why not tell me.

STENOGRAPHER. It was some mistake. It's sorted out, now, though. She's gone.

The STENOGRAPHER *sits and opens her notebook.*

LERMONTOV (*to* PALOCZI). So why not — *tell me?*

PALOCZI *is silent. Then a slight nod of his head towards the* STENOGRAPHER, *sitting with her pencil.*

Please leave us.

STENOGRAPHER. Beg pardon?

LERMONTOV. I said, please leave us for a moment.

STENOGRAPHER. But I was told —

LERMONTOV. Can't you hear what I am saying? Do I have to spell it out in semaphore? Please go away.

The STENOGRAPHER *goes. But on her way out, she overhears:*

They're some of them so slow and *stupid.* Villagers. They've never seen a city. So. Tell me. Why the peasants give away their food for free.

PALOCZI. You really want to know?

Slight pause.

LERMONTOV. It's my job to find out what is happening here.

Pause.

PALOCZI. Oh, well. Why not. What else have I to lose?

He takes off his hat, tosses it on the table, puts his feet up.

A dialectic, Comrade Lermontov. Thesis: 1947. I remember May Day. I was fourteen. Our liberation, from the landowners and counts. A real revolution, bubbling from below. Oh, very rushed and slapdash, but — still, real. And ours.

And then, antithesis, we found it wasn't ours, but yours. Sold to you cheap, bought from you dear. Your language and your culture papered over ours. And, if I may say so, your techniques of popular administration. And people felt betrayed. We felt betrayed .

LERMONTOV. And, synthesis?

PALOCZI. OK. A meeting. In a country town. All talk, and shouting, bickering and chaos; someone trying to organise a march on Budapest, they stopped that, someone else attempting to brew up tea on the bars of an electric fire. And a group of stolid peasants in some corner, furrowed brows, attempting to elect something or other; and they apologised, to me, I can't think why, that it was all taking such a time. You see, they hadn't actually elected anything before. They had to work out how to do it as they went along. And it was 1947 once again. And I thought, glory be. This time, it's actually real.

LERMONTOV. But communists were murdered.

PALOCZI. Were they?

LERMONTOV. Criminals and killers were set loose. Ordinary communists, good communists were lynched. Their hearts cut out.

PALOCZI. Maybe.

LERMONTOV. These things occurred.

Pause. PALOCZI *put his feet down.*

PALOCZI. Look. A revolution is a festival. Lenin said that, I was surprised to learn. And the thing about a festival is that it's very tricky to control. We have been drunk this last few weeks. For most of us, exhilaration. But for some, revenge. Mistakes get made. But the point is, that some crazy drunk stopped the collectivisation of the farms. And compulsory deliveries of food. And so the peasants loaded up their carts with everything that they could spare, and brought it here,

and gave it to the people. Because, at last, they trusted them.
    You know, I imagine, comrade, 1917 was very much a
festival.

LERMONTOV. You know, you're right. I think there's been an
error.

PALOCZI. Well —

LERMONTOV. I think you're the wrong man. You are not
Miklos Paloczi.

PALOCZI. Eh?

LERMONTOV. I think it's a mistake, and you should go.

He's marking the file. Quickly:

Go now. Go anywhere. You can still get to the border. Now!

PALOCZI *stands, his face is white.*

PALOCZI. Why, Comrade Lermontov?

LERMONTOV (*deliberately*). Because — I am of the view —
that revolutions should correct mistakes. If they are not to
lose the people's trust. And so — I'm trusting you.

Slight pause.

The border! Now!

PALOCZI (*blurted*). Will I get five yards beyond that door?

LERMONTOV. Maybe. Who knows?

PALOCZI. Give me your revolver.

LERMONTOV. You know I can't do that.

PALOCZI. I won't get far without it.

LERMONTOV. I can't go that far.

Slight pause. LERMONTOV *goes to the box of confiscated
weapons, and finds the grenade. He hands it to* PALOCZI.

Take that. It is — a sort of hand grenade.

PALOCZI *grins, puts his hat on, turns to go.*

How long?

PALOCZI. How — what?

LERMONTOV. For how long, do you think, will peasants give their food away? A month? A year? For ever?

Pause.

PALOCZI. Maybe. Who knows.

He looks at the grenade and smiles.

It's one of ours.

LERMONTOV *nods to the side door, and* PALOCZI *slips out.* LERMONTOV *makes another note on* PALOCZI's *file. There is a burst of gunfire from offstage.* LERMONTOV *looks towards it. Then, quickly, to the upstage area:*

LERMONTOV. Next!

TWO SOLDIERS *jab and shove the* 5TH PRISONER *into the office. He is extremely elegant, in his good overcoat and jewellery. He is* COUNT ISTVAN FORGACH. *The* SOLDIERS *go out.*

Russian?

Pause.

English?

Pause.

German?

FORGACH. Fluently.

LERMONTOV *looks at* FORGACH. *Then he looks through the files.*

LERMONTOV. Name.

FORGACH. I am Count Istvan Forgach.

LERMONTOV. Address?

FORGACH. Up until the 27th of October, the labour mines at Piliszentivan.

LERMONTOV. Since then?

FORGACH. The Gellert Hotel.

LERMONTOV. Occupation?

LERMONTOV *turns to* FORGACH, *having found the file.*
FORGACH *smiles.*

I mean, before.

FORGACH. Oh, I'd say . . . class enemy.

LERMONTOV. Are you a fascist?

FORGACH. Well . . .

A shruggy smile.

You know, before the war, we had a saying that seems to me
appropriate. Anti-semitism, it was said, is hating the Jews
more than is absolutely necessary.

LERMONTOV. What?

FORGACH. I'm a Hungarian.

A shout from outside.

VOICE: Help! Help me, please . . .

LERMONTOV. What's that?

A YOUNG SOLDIER *rushes into the upper area. He is badly
burnt. His hands in front of his face, his uniform ripped and
charred. He is followed by the* 1ST SOLDIER. *The* OTHER
SOLDIERS *rush to his aid, one turning back to cover the*
PRISONERS. *The* STENOGRAPHER *appears.*

YOUNG SOLDIER. Oh, Holy Mother help me.

LERMONTOV *towards the upper area, drawing a revolver.*

FORGACH. It appears to be some class of commotion.

1ST SOLDIER (*to* 2ND SOLDIER). A doctor, get a doctor,
quick.

The STENOGRAPHER *to the* YOUNG SOLDIER *as the*
2ND SOLDIER *runs out.*

YOUNG SOLDIER. Oh, no. God have mercy on me. Help me.
Please.

The STENOGRAPHER *and the* 1ST SOLDIER *help out the*
YOUNG SOLDIER. *We still hear him crying.* FORGACH
takes out a thin black cigar and lights it.

The STENOGRAPHER *re-enters to* LERMONTOV.

STENOGRAPHER. It's terrible. A barricade. And no one there. He stopped and opened up his tank, to take a look . . . They think, it was a young man with a hand-grenade . . .

LERMONTOV *turns, back into the office.*

FORGACH (*smiling, with a little wave*). Quite simple. God save Hungary.

LERMONTOV *shoots* FORGACH *twice.* FORGACH *slumps to the floor.* STENOGRAPHER *enters the office.*

STENOGRAPHER. What — happened?

LERMONTOV. Shot, while trying to escape.

Pause. The STENOGRAPHER *looks round.*

STENOGRAPHER. Where is — Where's the other one?

LERMONTOV. He wasn't who we thought he was. It was a mix-up. Such things happen. All the time.

STENOGRAPHER. There was some shooting, out there. Just before . . .

LERMONTOV. Apparently, they missed.

He strides out quickly. The STENOGRAPHER *looks at* FORGACH. *She realises he's still alive.*

FORGACH. Please. Help me.

Scene Three

Spring, 1962.
  The stage is empty. A seventeen-year old schoolboy, MARTIN GLASS, *stands alone in the middle of the parade ground of a minor public school. He wears army uniform, on which is prominently pinned the badge of the Campaign for Nuclear Disarmament. It is pouring with rain.* MARTIN *is dripping wet. He's been out here for some considerable time.*
  A SCHOOLMASTER *cycles on to the stage. He is* JEREMY CROWTHER. *He is thirty-three, he wears a black plastic mac and a black sou'wester. He cycles round, then cycles to*

MARTIN, *stops, and dismounts.*
   MARTIN *comes to attention.*

JEREMY. Uh — Glass, isn't it?

MARTIN. Glass, Martin B., yes, sir.

   Slight pause.

JEREMY. It's — pretty wet out here, Glass.

MARTIN. Yes, it is that, sir.

   Slight pause.

JEREMY. Now, you're in St Augustine, am I right?

MARTIN. No, sir. Sir Thomas More.

JEREMY. I see.

   Slight pause.

   Well, um, whatever, shouldn't you be there? I mean, parade
   fell out, what, best part of two hours ago.

   Slight pause.

   Glass, what are you doing here?

MARTIN. I was ordered to stay here, sir. After fall-out, sir. By
   Mr Sands. The adjutant.

JEREMY. Yes. Why?

MARTIN. Gross disrespect for the queen's uniform, sir.

   JEREMY *is forced to acknowledge* MARTIN's *badge.*

JEREMY. Oh, yes. Of course. Did Mr Sands give any indication
   of how long . . .

MARTIN. Till further notice, sir.

JEREMY. I see.

   Pause. JEREMY *looks up to the sky.*

   You know, it's quite interesting . . . The shape, I mean the
   actual construction of the symbol . . .

MARTIN. Is it, sir?

JEREMY. Yes. It's very clever, the, uh, two arms at the bottom, are the semaphore for N, nuclear, the top bit is the semaphore for D, disarmament, the middle as a whole's the broken cross, symbolic of the death of man, while the circle, you see, represents the unborn child . . . look, this is madness, you'll catch your death, I think you must come in.

MARTIN. Is that an order, sir?

JEREMY. Well, if you like.

MARTIN. It's not really a question of what I like.

JEREMY. All right, then. It's an order.

MARTIN (*to attention*). Sir!

Then MARTIN *breaks attention and makes to go.*

JEREMY. Look, Glass . . . Sir Thomas More is miles away. My cottage is just over there. I think you ought to get something hot inside you.

MARTIN *turns back to him.*

MARTIN. Yes, sir. Fucking right.

A transfer. MARTIN *leaves with the bicycle,* JEREMY *comes downstage and starts to take off his waterproofs, as a table and three chairs — on one of which hangs* MARTIN's *sodden uniform — are set up behind him.* JEREMY *calls offstage.*

JEREMY. So what did he say then?

MARTIN (*off*). Who, sir?

JEREMY. Mr Sands.

MARTIN (*off*). Oh, it wasn't so much 'say', sir, as 'harangue'. The matter of my class seemed to figure large. Apparently, my attitude to the H-bomb is a consequence of my people's income.

Enter MARTIN, *rubbing his hair with a towel.*

JEREMY. Why, are they very rich?

MARTIN. No, sir. My pa's a vicar. He's got a bit of private income, but it's been considerably eroded over recent years.

JEREMY. I'm sorry.

MARTIN. Well — his own fault, as it happens.

JEREMY. Oh. How so?

MARTIN. After the Sharpeville massacre, he insisted that we sell our shares in anything that had connections with South Africa. He didn't re-invest too wisely. Pretty tough to make ends meet.

JEREMY. Do you want some Horlicks?

MARTIN. You bet. Thanks.

He sits and sips a mug of Horlicks at the table.

JEREMY. Why do they keep you here, then?

MARTIN. Oh, I think . . . some sad, pathetic concept of propriety. My mother's concept, that is. She's a very proper woman. You know, the type who thinks the *dolce vita's* something you look up in Baedeker.

JEREMY laughs.

I mean, like the vicarage is next door to a US Air Force base, bang in the fucking firing line, so she supports the annihilation of the species as a simple point of social etiquette. You know.

JEREMY laughs again.

I mean they've got a 1957 Morris Oxford. And when they come to Speech Day, she insists they park it half a mile away and walk. So as not to Show Me Up, As if I cared.

JEREMY. You sound as if you care.

MARTIN. Well, it makes me angry. My mother, trying to ape those people who could buy us up, and all we've got, and not bother with the change.

JEREMY (*with a gesture to the badge on* MARTIN's *tunic*). And that? That makes you angry too?

MARTIN. Not in the same way, no, sir. That is because it's right. As I imagine you think too.

JEREMY. Well, as it happens, I have sat down in my time.

MARTIN. Gosh, have you, sir? And been arrested?

JEREMY. Nearly. Twice.

> *During this speech,* MARTIN *takes out ten cigarettes, and a box of matches. He takes out a cigarette and opens the matches. They are sodden.* JEREMY *looking on in some panic.*

MARTIN. Then I imagine you'd resent as much as I do the idea you want to ban the bomb because you want to kill your mother. Kind of, kindergarten Freud, I imagine you'd regard it, sir.

JEREMY. Well, yes.

MARTIN. Look, sir. I'm sorry, but it has been quite a day. Do you have a light?

JEREMY. A light?

> MARTIN *rattles the damp matches.*

Look, strictly speaking . . .

> *As he finds a box of matches and gives them to* MARTIN, *lamely:*

They're terribly bad for you.

MARTIN (*lighting up*). I'm always keen to see, sir, how far people are prepared to go.

JEREMY. Well, are you now.

MARTIN. And in your case, sir, it's particularly interesting to me, how you end up here at all.

JEREMY. Why's that?

MARTIN. Being a communist, and so on.

> *Pause.*

JEREMY. Um . . .

MARTIN. Bit of a turn up for the books, I'd say.

JEREMY. What makes you —

MARTIN. Wavish, Roger P., in Kant, has this pa who was a red at Trinity. For a birthday present, he gave me a copy of the *Daily Worker* for the day that I was born. May the second, 1945.

Slight pause.

I assume that you're the same J.H. Crowther, sir?
'Throughout the continent, the toiling masses rise'?

Pause.

JEREMY. Well —

MARTIN. I mean, a ban-the-bomber, you could be a Methodist
or a vegetarian or something. But actually in The Party.
Wavish and I view that as really cool.

Pause.

JEREMY. Well, I'm afraid I'm not in it any more.

MARTIN. Why not, sir?

JEREMY. Because I left it over Hungary.

Slight pause.

Well, more accurately, I left it at the time of Hungary. It was
actually 'over' what were called my 'obstinately opportunist
tendencies'. Or, put another way . . . Look, is this of any
interest at all?

MARTIN (*sweetly*). Oh, very much so, sir.

Slight pause.

JEREMY. Well, it was really very simple. They sent this
apparatchik up, to explain the line. Those brave, wild
revolutionaries in the streets of Budapest, 'objectively' the
agents of imperialism. And I thought then — oh, come on, do
you really want this man to run the country? And I left. And
it was — just like that.

MARTIN. And you ended up —

JEREMY (*sharply*). I picked this place out with a pin. It seemed
a reasonable alternative to busking in the Underground,
that's all.

MARTIN. But, really? Just Like That?

Pause.

JEREMY. All right, then. Look. I didn't go to Trinity. In fact,

I was born in Halifax. And although my family would not
have known an opportunist tendency had one leant over and
bit them — in fact they thought that reading stunted growth
— we all knew people who had elder brothers, fathers,
friends, who were either near or in the Party. And some of
them, the best of them, went off to Spain. And the very best
of those did not come back.

And so when *we* came of age, when it was all over, the
thirties, and the war, we had this feeling we were fifteen
years too young. And I tell you, there's no stranger feeling
than the feeling that instead of being past it, it's past you.

And what we'd missed, of course, was all the glory. All
that certainty, that once you'd cracked the shackles of the
system, every man indeed would be an Aristotle or a
Michelangelo. Because in a way, it had already happened.
And it hadn't turned out how we thought it would at all. Oh,
it was decent, sure, and reasonably caring, in its bureaucratic
way . . . And indeed there was full employment and high
wages and although there was still some miserable poverty,
there was less of it than there'd ever been before . . . And, for
us, of course, we did particularly well, there were
scholarships, and places at the less pretentious redbrick
universities, and some of us wrote poetry, and others novels,
and some were published, and some not . . . And we worked
on literary magazines, or the Third Programme, or we
didn't . . .

But you realise there's something missing. The working
class is freer than it's ever been. But somewhere, in the
no-man's-land between private affluence and public squalor,
somewhere inside the Hoover Automatic or the Mini-Cooper,
behind the television or underneath the gramophone, those
wonderful possessions . . . You hear a kind of scream. The
scream of the possessed.

And you realise there's all the difference in the world,
between liberty and liberation.

MARTIN *has taken a manuscript from his pocket.*

JEREMY (*a glance at his watch*). Now look, old boy —

MARTIN *suddenly jumps on a chair and reads his manuscript:*

MARTIN. And like a peace bomb a still gentle bomb a shalom bomb a non-bomb a still small voice on the switchback a still sane whisper on the wheel

Written on walls of houses fallen written amid bomb site rubble in the spaces in the skyline

Tattooed on the translucent flesh of the children of the ashes the daughters of the dustbowl the class of August 1945

Carved in the gravestones of the nations of the dead and etched like acid on the frontal lobes of the poisoned gnomes who live beneath the earth the Kremlin gremlins and the Penta-megamen

Etcetera, etcetera . . .

The single word — Resist.

He gets down.

It's called *Beyond.* I'm aware that it's derivative. But I imagine I'll grow out of that. The title's after Sartre. He said that he was only interested, now, in what lies beyond despair.

He looks at JEREMY.

Not bang in the middle of it, Mr Crowther.

JEREMY. Well. I suppose — touché.

MARTIN *takes off the dressing-gown and gets dressed.*

MARTIN. You see, I think —

JEREMY. Yes, what?

MARTIN. For you, sir, the mass of people seem to be, just victims. Passive and inert. To be pitied, yes, to be the object of your agonised compassion . . . But basically, a lump of stodge. Whereas, in my view, there will come a time, when you'll hear that scream in unison. And when you do, when they've really cracked the shackles of the system for themselves — who knows how many Michelangelos could bloom?

He makes to go.

JEREMY. You're right. Of course.

MARTIN. I'm sorry, sir?

JEREMY. Oh, yes. But perhaps, who knows, there'll come a time we'll find some brave wild kids on *our* side of the wire, who'll do it, really get it right. *This* time.

You see, it wasn't 'just like that'. In fact, it smashed my life.

Pause.

MARTIN. Sir, I do think I understand. I'm sure that, if I was you, I'd wish I'd been a red — at Trinity or anywhere — who'd been to Spain.

He turns and goes. JEREMY *looks at the poem, which* MARTIN *left on the table.*

JEREMY. 'And even to be glimpsed behind the tired and chicken-wired eyes of those who cannot quite remember what it was to feel alive . . .'

He looks up. To himself:

Not 'just like that', remotely.

Scene Four

A railway track in Northern California. Summer, 1967. The track runs upstage/downstage. A young man with a bullhorn, CLARK SULLIVAN. *He shouts at a group of anti-draft* PROTESTERS:

CLARK. Let's go let's go let's go let's go let's go.

The PROTESTERS *run and sit on the track, downstage.* MARTIN *at the side.* CLARK *to the stragglers, including* MARTIN:

Let's *go.*

MARTIN *runs to join the* PROTESTERS *sitting on the track as the train enters from upstage centre. It judders to a halt a few feet from the* PROTESTERS.

Now we don't have too much time here, people. Everyone link arms. If you don't know the person next to you, say hi.

To two MALE PROTESTERS:

Hey, give us a hand up here.

As CLARK *is hoisted on to the two* PROTESTER'*s shoulders,* MARTIN *speaks to the* YOUNG WOMAN *next to him.*

MARTIN. Hallo. I'm Martin Glass.

CATHY. Hi there. I'm Cathy Weiner.

MARTIN. I'm from Britain.

CATHY. You don't say.

CLARK *speaking upstage, towards the train, through the bullhorn:*

CLARK. Good morning, fellow Americans. I am speaking to you on behalf of the Butch Cassidy Division of the Bay Area Brigade of the Draft Resisters International.

MARTIN. Who is this guy?

CATHY. His name's Clark Sullivan. He's big in the Movement round these parts.

MARTIN. Well, so it would appear.

CLARK. We have stopped your train in order to tell you why we think you should quit the army now and refuse to fight their scabby, skunky little war.

CATHY. His father's the President of Petroleum Incorporated of Connecticut. His mother's in the DAR. He's into smashing American Imperialism.

MARTIN. Yes.

CLARK. You been told by the Man that you're going out there to kill a lot of little yellow people dressed in black pyjamas who could not eat shit. Well, we're here to tell you that those ginks out there are winning. And the only ass that's going to get kicked is yours.

CATHY. Oh-oh.

NATIONAL GUARDSMEN, *wearing gasmasks, running in and forming a line either side of the track.* CLARK *turns to the* PROTESTERS.

CLARK. 'There does come a time.'

PROTESTERS. There comes a time.

CLARK. When the operation of the machine —

PROTESTERS. When the operation of the machine —

CLARK. Becomes so odious —

PROTESTERS. So odious —

CLARK. Makes you sick at heart —

PROTESTERS. So sick at heart —

CLARK. That you can't take part, and you've got to put your bodies on the gears —

PROTESTERS. The gears!

CLARK. And on the wheels —

PROTESTERS. The wheels!

CLARK. On the levers, on all the apparatus —

PROTESTERS. All the apparatus!

CLARK. And you've got to make it stop.

The NATIONAL GUARDSMEN *are in place. Silence.*

OK now, boys and girls. For the next five minutes, we have got to be like the Panthers. Be like the freedom fighters of the world. We must be the Vietnamese.

Pause. The clink and clunk of tear gas cannisters being loaded into launchers. MARTIN *whispers.*

MARTIN. What happens now?

CATHY. Well, I guess there'll be some tear-gas. And they'll move in, I'd imagine, with their night-sticks. And it's ten to one we'll all get busted, and we'll all get hurt.

MARTIN. And then?

CATHY. I guess — we stop the war.

Slight pause.

Have you seen *The Battle of Algiers?*

OFFICER. Fire!

Launchers fired. The stage fills with smoke. The
GUARDSMEN *move in. Then, darkness.*

Scene Five

In the darkness, the voice of JAMES GRAIN, *through a*
microphone.

JAMES. Comrades, my name is Grain, and I'm on the Central
Committee of an organisation called Socialist Vanguard.

Lights on.
   A meeting hall in a students union in the Midlands, May
1968. JAMES GRAIN *is thirty-five.*

Comrades, this is an extraordinary meeting, and it is a
measure of the extraordinary epoch through which we are
moving. As countless speakers have stated here today, we
have witnessed, over the last five months, events that would
have seemed unthinkable even a year ago. The Tet offensive
of the National Liberation Front in Vietnam. The *de facto*
resignation of the President of the United States. Most of all,
today, in France, not just ten thousand students but ten
million workers pose a challenge, not only to this policy or
that, or even to this government or that, but to the power
and legitimacy of the state itself. And we can see it even
here.

   But, comrades, forgive me for one note of caution.
Comrades, read the writing on the wall.

He gestures to the banners that we imagine are hung around
the hall.

'Don't demand: occupy.' Yes, that's fine. And 'Victory to
the NLF.' That's good as well, that's right, we don't want
peace in Vietnam, but victory.

   'The Revolution is the Festival of the Oppressed.' That's
very good indeed. But in fact, it's only half the story.

   It's a quote from Lenin. Yes, I'm afraid so, Lenin. Let me

read the whole of it to you.

He reads:

'Revolutions are festivals of the oppressed and exploited . . .
At such times the people are capable of performing miracles.
But we shall be traitors and betrayers of the revolution, if
we do not use the festive energy of the masses to wage a
ruthless and self-sacrificing struggle for the direct and
decisive path . . .'

    What is that path? Where should we go? To coin another
slogan: What Is To Be Done?

Pause. He looks round.

Let me explain.

Scene Six

*And old house in the Midlands, May 1968. Mid-evening. Upstage
is a sitting-room area, with old furniture, a black and white TV
set, sleeping bags. Downstage is the eating part of the kitchen: a
table, chairs, a washing line with nappies, a plastic clothes
basket.*

    Between the two areas, an old duplicator on which PHIL *is
running off a leaflet. He's twenty, from Birmingham. The
duplicator run finishes.* PHIL *removes the stencil as* CLARK
SULLIVAN *enters with a rucksack. He puts it down.* PHIL *is
standing with the inky stencil and its backing sheet, not
knowing what to do.* CLARK *goes to the clothes line, takes
down a nappy, tosses it in the plastic basket, and clips the
stencil on to the clothes line.*

PHIL. Ah. Smart thinking.

CLARK. Don't mention it. How many pages?

PHIL. Eight or nine.

    CLARK *takes all the nappies down, and puts them in the
basket.*

    Even smarter.

    PHIL *sees the rucksack.*

Where are you off to?

CLARK. California.

PHIL (*not really listening*). Oh, ar?

> PHIL *putting a new stencil on.* CLARK *takes an envelope from his pocket, and clips that, too, on to the clothes line. Then he picks up the rucksack and goes out.* PHIL *tries to start the machine.*

> Oh, come on. Just for mother, eh?

> *He kicks the machine. It starts.*

> I love you.

> *As* PHIL *takes the already duplicated pages from the basket, kneels on the floor and lays them out to collate,* AMANDA *enters from another part of the house, with a tray of dirty mugs. She notes the duplicator, the stencil on the line, but not, as he is obscured,* PHIL. AMANDA *is twenty-one.*

AMANDA. I don't believe this.

> PHIL *pops his head up.*

PHIL. So then, what d'you think?

AMANDA. Of what?

PHIL. The Roneo. I got it, knock down, from the Catholic Association. I wasn't sure they'd take to selling off their surplus to the Socialist Society, so I told 'em I was from the Hockey Club. Apparently, they needed cash for a trip to Lourdes.

> *The machine stops.*

> They could have taken this along as well.

> *He hits the machine. It goes.*

> Ave Maria.

> *Enter* MARTIN *from the street. He now wears a moustache.*

AMANDA. Martin.

MARTIN. Amanda.

AMANDA (*taking the tray into the kitchen*). How was the conference?

MARTIN. Weren't you there?

AMANDA (*off*). Of course I wasn't there. I was dragging Tania all round fucking Lipton's, wasn't I?

MARTIN. Par for the course. Maoists all morning, Trots all afternoon.

AMANDA (*off*). Which Trots?

MARTIN. SV.

>   AMANDA *reappears.* PHIL *changing the stencil.*

AMANDA. Take care, sir. You speak of the Party I love.

MARTIN. I know.

>   CATHY *appears from elsewhere in the house. She wears a jacket over a nightie, and woolly socks. She goes through to the kitchen, singing.*

CATHY. 'All the leaves are brown, all the leaves are brown, and the sky is grey . . .'

>   *She has gone.*

AMANDA. Now, where are the Leeds Two, I wonder?

>   *Doorbell.*

Ah. They've lost another key.

>   *She goes to answer the door. During the following,* CATHY *appears with a plate of raw vegetables, goes to the upstage area, sits, and reads a book as she eats.*

PHIL. Red Barcelona. Spanish Civil War.

MARTIN. Beg pardon?

PHIL. Cautionary tale. In 1937, Catalonia. The anarchists collectivised the factories, the farms, the trains, the cinemas, the stores. Even the greyhound tracks. But then the communists decided that the Revolution had to wait, in the interests of defeating Franco, and the anarchists were smashed. By the communists, that is. Five Days in May. Five hundred dead.

MARTIN. Point, Phil.

PHIL. The CP, 1937. The SV, 1968. In my view, anyway. Same glint. Same steely eye. Same cast of mind.

MARTIN (*helping* PHIL *with his duplicating*). Well, my basic problem with the Socialist Vanguard is more prosaic. It's that, if you want to be a member, they tell you the ten funniest jokes in the history of the world —

PHIL. And if you don't smile once —

PHIL.   ⎫
           ⎬ You're in.
MARTIN. ⎭

> AMANDA *has brought in* JAMES GRAIN.

JAMES. Good evening. I'm James Grain.

MARTIN. Oh, yes. Hallo.

JAMES. And I assure you, I'm a laugh a minute.

AMANDA. Sit down, James.

JAMES. Thank you.

> JAMES *sits at the table.* PHIL *returns to his work.*

And you are Martin Glass.

> *A bang at the door. Enter* BRIAN *and* JUDY. *They are students from Leeds.*

BRIAN. Hi, Mand.

JUDY. Hi, Mand.

AMANDA, Hi, Bri. Hi, Jude.

JUDY. Hi, Mart.

MARTIN. Hi, Jude. Hi, Bri.

BRIAN. Hi, Phil.

PHIL. Hi, Bri.

JUDY. Hey, news.

BRIAN. Yur, right.

JUDY. Hi, Cath.

CATHY (*waving*). Hi, hi.

> BRIAN *puts on the television.*

JAMES. I'm finding this a bit hard to work out.

> *We see the flicker of the television on the faces of* BRIAN *and* JUDY, *who are watching the Nine O'Clock News.*

AMANDA. Brian and Judy are from Leeds, for the conference. Martin and Phil are my permanent lodgers. Cathy and Clark are my temporary lodgers. Clark is evading conscription, and so Martin sweetly told him he could crash. Martin met them in America. He spent a summer out there. Way out.

JAMES. Yes, I know. I read his pieces in — what was it? *Insurrection?*

MARTIN. *Stick Up.*

JAMES. Yes. Led me to think, in fact, it might be time you joined.

MARTIN. I'm not exactly what you'd call a joiner.

JAMES. Then perhaps you're not exactly what I'd call a revolutionary.

> *Pause.*

MARTIN. Which party would you recommend?

JAMES. Socialist Vanguard is a revolutionary grouping of militant youth, students, intellectuals and above all, workers. We are not to be confused with the Socialist Alliance, from whom we split, or the Left Opposition, who split from us, or Workers' Struggle, who split from them, or with the League for Revolutionary Socialism, who never split at all, they just burn people out, hence the ten funniest jokes joke, which was first used about them when you were still in nappies. We should also be distinguished, in passing, from the Revolutionary Marxist Fraction, the International Communist Current, and the Marxist Workers' Tendency. All clear so far?

MARTIN. Yes. Absolutely. What's the difference?

JAMES. They're wrong and we're right.

MARTIN. Right about what?

JAMES. Well, where to start.

> *Pause.* JAMES *gives a slight nod to* AMANDA, *who goes upstage. She watches television, but with half an ear on* MARTIN *and* JAMES' *conversation.*

> I'd say — primarily — we're right in being internationalists. In ascribing the failure of the Soviet Revolution — and indeed of the other revolutions made in its image — to the Stalinist betrayal, the attempt to build socialism in one country. And we're right too to believe that what is going on today in almost every Western country — what you describe so elegantly in your articles about America — is in many ways a genuinely revolutionary phenomenon.

MARTIN. Well, good.

JAMES. The rejection of the centralised rigidities of old left politics.

MARTIN. I'd go along with that.

JAMES. The creation in their stead of a new left politics in which the means and ends of revolution are the same.

MARTIN. Well, I couldn't put it better my —

JAMES. A politics defined primarily by the belief that it is possible to build the New Jerusalem within the very belly of the monster, not in the future, but in the here-and-now.

MARTIN. I think, in fact, that's how I put it. Glad that you agree.

JAMES. I think, in fact, about your articles, the word I used was 'elegant'.

> *Pause.*

MARTIN. Go on.

JAMES. Well, the fact is, for a start, that in your articles, you used the word 'working', as an adjective preceding 'class', precisely once. In a sentence full, as I recall, of dismissive references to motor-cars and Hoover Automatics.

Slight pause.

MARTIN. Yes, I see.

JAMES. Not sure you do. Look. For twenty years or so, the myth's been growing that the Western working class has been bought off, sucked in, and that the future for the Revolution lay with peasants in Bolivia, or blacks in the cities of America, or students, or communards in San Francisco or Vermont, or with anyone, except the working class. In many learned volumes, in many different ways. But do you know what's happening? Catastrophe. The workers haven't got round to reading all these worthy tomes. They haven't heard they've been sucked in. Someone forgot to tell them, obviously, and so ten million of them, silly fools, are out on strike in France today.

MARTIN. Sparked off by whom?

JAMES. Oh, the students. Absolutely. The disaffected young. The freaks, the anarchists. But it didn't end there, and it *couldn't* end there. Which is why we're in the business of turning freaks and anarchists and hippies into revolutionary socialists, and not the other way round.

MARTIN. You mean, turn.

He makes the peace sign — Churchill's Victory-V

to

He makes the clenched-fist sign.

JAMES. Well, if you like.

MARTIN. Not sure I do.

JAMES. Then do ask yourself the question, if we don't, where they will be in five years time, when the carnival is over, and it's back to the long haul? Where will *you* be?

MARTIN. I'm sorry, I don't understand.

JAMES. They will find that in the long-term it just doesn't work. That, ultimately, all the communes and collectives and co-operatives do not confront the basic issue of the ownership of capital. And when they realise that violence and greed and xenophobia are not the products of men's minds but of their circumstances, they will either drift away, so slowly they don't notice, or they'll take revenge upon the inadequacies of the world by turning to the bullet and the bomb, the weapons of despair.

So it is legitimate to ask of them, of you, of everyone who claims to be a revolutionary: what sacrifices are *you* prepared to make, to prove that you're a real traitor to your class, that you're not just — on holiday?

Pause. MARTIN *suddenly turns, goes upstage and out.*
AMANDA *stands there.*

AMANDA. Well, I suppose — it's only rock and roll.

JAMES *comes upstage.*

JAMES. What's going on?

BRIAN. Troop movements outside Paris. And they've stopped Cohn-Bendit coming back to France.

JUDY. And the CGT have prevented students talking to the Citroen workers.

BRIAN. Renault.

JUDY. Sorry.

BRIAN. Renault-Billancourt.

AMANDA. And the CP says the situation isn't revolutionary.

BRIAN. Well, that's it, back to Ronan Point.

AMANDA *switches off the television.*

PHIL. Just watch it all come down.

PHIL *goes back to his duplicator.*

CATHY (*suddenly*). Hey, has anyone seen Clark?

Head-shaking. PHIL *doesn't hear until during:*

You know, big guy, with the moustache and the long hair and the funny accent? Must have noticed him around —

PHIL. Here, earlier. Said, going out.

CATHY. Out where?

PHIL. Um . . .

CATHY. Jesus.

PHIL. Colchester.

CATHY. Where's Colchester?

PHIL. Or Canterbury? Something. Ca. I'm sorry. Somewhere, sounds like 'California'.

JAMES (*to* AMANDA). I ought to go.

CATHY. Like *California?*

> JAMES *goes to pick up his file.* CATHY *rapidly goes out, bumping into the re-entering* MARTIN. MARTIN *has some documents.*

> Excuse *me.*

> *She is gone.* MARTIN *quickly to* JAMES *at the table.*

MARTIN. My father is a clergyman. He doles out opiate to the masses three times every Sunday. And his father had a little money, and when I was twenty-one, a portion of it came to me.

> *He takes out a lighter and sets fire to the documents, which are share certificates.*

Phoenix Assurance, ordinary, 50, British Petroleum, ordinary, 25 —

> *The* OTHERS *reacting.*

AMANDA. Hey, Martin —

MARTIN. Unigate Dairies, preferential, 60, Beechams —

> AMANDA *runs into the kitchen.*

PHIL. Jesus Christ.

MARTIN. Ordinary, 70 —

JUDY. What's going on?

MARTIN. The estimated value of the whole portfolio —

> AMANDA *rushes back in with a saucepan of water.*

AMANDA. For God's sake, put that lot in here —

MARTIN. Two thousand, seven hundred —

AMANDA grabs the flaming certificates and throws them in the saucepan.

AMANDA. There.

Pause.

PHIL. Hey, wow.

Pause.

JAMES. You idiot. If you hadn't wanted them, you should have given them to us.

Pause. PHIL, BRIAN *and* JUDY *return upstage.*

MARTIN. I'm sorry. That was quite ridiculous.

JAMES. In fact, you can write off, and they'll send you duplicates.

Slight pause.

I'm just sorry that you missed the point, that's all.

MARTIN. What do you mean?

CATHY re-enters hurriedly. Her brow furrowed, she looks round the room. Then she sees the note on the washing line. She goes over, opens it and reads, as:

JAMES. I mean that I frankly couldn't give a toss about your guilty conscience, I don't even care if you're repressing latent homosexuality, or if you really want to kill your mother. All that bothers me, and the point that I was trying to make, is that until you purge that guilt, until you sacrifice your individual conscience, then you will be frankly useless to the business which now faces us.

MARTIN. Which is?

JAMES. The building of a party strong and hard and disciplined enough to provide at least the means whereby the masses can seize human history. That's all.

MARTIN (*suddenly, to* AMANDA). Do you agree with this?

AMANDA. Yes. Yes, of course I do.

Pause. CATHY *has read the note. In it, a pendant on a chain.*

CATHY. You shit.

(*To* PHIL). You shit. You . . . Fucking Canterbury.

She runs into the kitchen.

PHIL. Obviously wrong.

Pause.

AMANDA. Martin. It would be wonderful if it could all be nice.
Make love not war. CND marchers, singing 'We Shall
Overcome', as they shuffle through a dripping English Easter
afternoon. But there comes a point, there really does, when
you have to think about the other side.

JAMES. Hear hear.

AMANDA. Like, my father-in-law is in the building trade.
Employs three men. And treats them better than he treats
himself. How could it possibly be moral, right or good, to
take that firm away from him? But the point is that that
little firm is just the bottom of a pyramid. And at the top sit
General Motors, Boeing, Standard Oil and Chase Manhattan.
And he understands that if they go, he goes. And there are
millions like him. Who come the crunch will take up arms,
will fight and maim and kill, to keep that pyramid in place.

JAMES. Yes. There is that phrase of Trotsky's.

MARTIN. What's that?

JAMES. Human dust.

Pause.

PHIL. Red Barcelona.

Pause.

MARTIN. Yes.

He turns to BRIAN *and* JUDY.

Now, look, it's ten to ten, does anybody fancy one before
they close?

CATHY *has reappeared. She's still very angry. She has the
note in one hand, the pendant in the other.*

CATHY. Now I have, before you guys depart. To raise a certain
matter.

Slight pause.

It's about my grapefruit. Now to you, it may be just a yellow, spherical . . . But it's kind of vital to my dietary requirements. Do you dig? I mean, I have to eat a half a grapefruit every half a day.

Slight pause.

Now, you people mustn't get me wrong here. The communal life. Right on. But I'll thank you, nonetheless . . . I'll thank you all . . . to leave my food alone.

Pause.

AMANDA. We're talking about grapefruit?

CATHY. Yes.

Pause. She crumples the note in her hand.

He wants to be the fucking Vietcong. Petroleum Incorporated. Joining up. To be the fucking Santa Barbara division of the Vietcong.

Pause. She plays the pendant through her fingers.

Burn baby burn.
To Bring The War On Home.

Pause. She bangs her temple with the flat of her hand.

Please excuse me.

She goes out.

JUDY. Bri, you go.

BRIAN. Beg pardon?

JUDY. Shan't be long. You go.

JUDY goes out after CATHY. *Pause.*

PHIL. Her dad was in the Party in the thirties. Lot of guilt there. Lot of mess. Hard to snap your fingers, will it all away.

He goes out with MARTIN, *to the street.* BRIAN *follows.* JAMES *and* AMANDA *left alone.*

JAMES. I think I must go now.

AMANDA. Oh, must you?

JAMES. Catch the last train. I've a meeting, early in the morning.

AMANDA. Well, of course.

Pause.

I've got some scotch, I think, in case you'd like one for the road.

JAMES. Well, that might be very nice.

AMANDA *goes into the kitchen, returning with half a bottle of scotch and two glasses. She pours.*

AMANDA. And in fact . . . In fact, there is a train at 7.30 in the morning. Gets you into London, oh, by half past nine.

Slight pause.

If you should care to . . .

JAMES. Well, that might be even nicer.

AMANDA *gives* JAMES *his scotch.*

Father-in-law?

AMANDA. We separated. Shortly after Tania —

JAMES. Yes.

Pause.

AMANDA. Let's go and fuck, OK?

She walks upstage, JAMES *following, as* MARTIN *burst back in.*

MARTIN. Look —

AMANDA *and* JAMES *stop.*

Look, the point is, that I didn't mean . . .

He clocks some of the situation.

But I have decided. No.

Slight pause.

JAMES. Well, history will have to muddle on without you, Martin.

He looks to AMANDA, *who gestures the direction of the stairs.* JAMES *goes out.* AMANDA *follows.* MARTIN *left alone.*

Scene Seven

Red Square, Moscow. August 1968.
A couple of POLICEMEN. *Two men downstage. One is a*
rather dusty-looking man of thirty-five or so, a cigarette hanging
from his mouth. His name is PUGACHEV. *The other man is*
LERMONTOV, *now thirty-nine.*

LERMONTOV. Comrade Pugachev.

PUGACHEV. Comrade Lermontov.

LERMONTOV. Leonid Sergeyevich, doctor of philology,
   candidate member, the Academy of Sciences.

PUGACHEV (*not sure of the point*). Pavel Mikhailovich,
   translator, the Institute of African and Asian Peoples. What is
   going on?

LERMONTOV (*striding off*). We are going on a scientific
   expedition.

PUGACHEV (*following, unhappily*). In Red Square?

LERMONTOV. That's right. Because this is where it happened.

PUGACHEV. Speaking in English?

LERMONTOV. They will think it is some obscure Islamic
   dialect. They will think we are tourists from Tadzhikistan.

PUGACHEV. Tourists don't do this.

LERMONTOV. This is the first place.

PUGACHEV. I have never seen a tourist doing this.

LERMONTOV. This is the position of the pram, wheeled by the
   poetess. Who meets the other six, who have converged on the
   square from different directions, choosing this spot because
   it's nowhere near a traffic lane.

   Pause.

PUGACHEV. I see.

LERMONTOV. The poetess reaches under the mattress of the
   pram — under her baby — and produces banners. One bears
   the ancient Polish slogan: 'For your freedom — and for ours'.

PUGACHEV (*making to go*). Yes, fine, Pavel —

LERMONTOV. And if you take another step, I will shout out what the other banner said, in Russian.

PUGACHEV *stops*.

PUGACHEV. All right. Just make it quick.

LERMONTOV. They sit here, on the ground. A whistle blows. KGB men, in civilian clothes, rush from all sides.

PUGACHEV (*looking round warily*). Yes, they have a tendency to do that.

LERMONTOV. As they run, they shout: 'Look at those Jews and traitors!'

PUGACHEV. And that too.

LERMONTOV. The art historian is here, when they hit him in the face and break his teeth. The physicist is here, when they hit him with a heavy suitcase. The cars arrive there, there and there, and take the six away. The mother and her baby sit here for ten minutes, till they come and take her too. They beat her in the car. The other slogan reads: 'Hands off Czechoslovakia'.

Pause.

PUGACHEV. Yes, of course I heard about it. There was a meeting at the Institute, to condemn the hooligans.

LERMONTOV. I am assembling a petition.

PUGACHEV. Comparisons were drawn with those student anarchists who used to read out dirty poetry in Mayakovsky Square. Schoolboys, attention seekers, juvenile delinquents.

LERMONTOV. The petition quotes the Soviet Constitution, Article one hundred twenty-five —

PUGACHEV. Look, Pavel, I'm sure it's all a terrible mistake —

LERMONTOV. I was in Hungary. I was sure that was a terrible mistake. Till I saw it happening again.

Pause.

PUGACHEV. I don't think I've ever seen you quite this angry.

LERMONTOV. I have been quite this angry only twice before. Once was in Hungary. The other was when I learnt about my father.

Slight pause. PUGACHEV *looks miserable.*

He'd joined the Komsomol in 1923. In 1931, he volunteered to help collectivise the peasantry. And when he realised that what that actually meant was helping to annihilate the peasantry, he was arrested, charged and tried for 'insufficient revolutionary vigilance'.

PUGACHEV. Uh — was he — ?

LERMONTOV. No, as it happens, he was rehabilitated, just in time to die defending Leningrad. It had all been 'a terrible mistake'.

Slight pause.

PUGACHEV. Look, can we go now, please, Pavel?

LERMONTOV. My petition reads —

PUGACHEV. I'm afraid my memories are less, dramatic.

LERMONTOV. To the Procurator General, the Union —

PUGACHEV. I just remember living with three other families in a freezing room divided by old sheets hung from the ceiling. And being hungry from the age of eight to the age of seventeen.
    Look, of course I'm on their side.
    But a demonstration, seen by no one. Lasting 20 seconds. Now, that is just — ridiculous.
    I'm so sorry, Pavel Mikhailovich.

He goes. The POLICEMEN *look at* LERMONTOV.
LERMONTOV *takes a paper from his pocket. He unfolds it. It's a map.*

LERMONTOV (*to the* POLICEMEN). I think — I'm lost.

Scene Eight

A corridor in a building in Leeds University. October, 1969. A sprayed slogan: THE UNIVERSITY OF LIFE. Off the corridor, an office, with a desk. On it, a telephone, and a certain amount of mess, paper cups, beer cans, etc. JEREMY is in the corridor, looking at the slogan. He wears an overcoat, and carries a briefcase and a copy of 'The Times'. A knot of STUDENTS, a little way away, in animated discussion.

JEREMY. Sadly, in fact, the University of Leeds.

JEREMY *turns to go into the office. One of the* STUDENTS *notices* JEREMY. *It's* JUDY.

JUDY. What the hell — (*Coming over to* JEREMY.) Excuse me, 'scuse me —

JEREMY. Yes?

JUDY. Who are you?

JEREMY. My name is Crowther. I teach English Studies. This is my office. Who are you?

JUDY. Can I ask you, how you got in here?

JEREMY. I walked in.

JUDY. Through the lobby?

JEREMY. No, the mezzanine. It's easier, from where I park my car. Why d'you ask?

JUDY (*calls to the other* STUDENTS). The mezzanine!

A couple of STUDENTS *rush out. Another* STUDENT — *it's* BRIAN — *comes over to* JEREMY *and* JUDY.

JUDY. I'm sorry, but you shouldn't have got in. The building's occupied.

JEREMY. I see. By whom?

JUDY. By us.

JEREMY. Who's us?

JUDY. The student's union.

JEREMY. I thought you had a building of your own.

Very slight pause.

I'm sorry, what I mean is —

BRIAN. Hi. The reason for this occupation is that the University is allowing military recruitment on campus. Specifically, the TA has a stall here, for the freshers, in the lobby of this building. Please — do have a leaflet.

JEREMY. Thank you.

BRIAN. Not at all.

JEREMY. Well, now, look, I'm sure it's most objectionable —

JEREMY *looking at the leaflet, as he speaks.*

BRIAN. Then why don't you object?

JEREMY. But I have got three months mail . . . And a class to give, as well . . .

BRIAN. I rather doubt if they'll turn up.

JEREMY. And actually —

JUDY. Oh, go on, teacher. Be a traitor to your class.

JEREMY (*snaps*). Are you aware . . . that, in this document, you have, at a cursory glance, split four infinitives?

JUDY *and* BRIAN *look at each other.*

And are you, I just ask for information, actually serious in claiming that this — seat of learning is 'a velvet glove, wrapped round the fist of neo-fascism'?

Slight pause.

That's f-a-s-*h*-i-s-m?

JUDY. Look, it's very simple. Military recruitment —

JEREMY (*moving to the door at his office*). Yes, I fully understand the *casus belli*, but I must insist —

JUDY (*blocking* JEREMY). Beg pardon? *Casus* what?

JUDY *and* JEREMY *glare at each other.*

JEREMY. It's an expression, taken from the Latin. Latin is a language, spoken many years ago in Italy —

JUDY. My pa was in the war. Conscripted, from a back-to-back in Huddersfield. He didn't see an inside tap till he was seventeen. At 19 half his face was blown away, on a beach in Normandy called Gold.

You take one step, I'll kick your balls in, sir.

Pause.

JEREMY. I fought for this. I fought for you. Wrote articles. Gave evidence to commissions. To cut a clearing in the groves of academe, for People Just Like You.

BRIAN. Well, thanks a bunch.

JEREMY. But a demonstration, in a corridor. Now that is just — ridiculous.

JUDY. I'm sorry, Mr Crowther.

A STUDENT *runs in.*

STUDENT. Hey. Pigs, swarming through the fucking mezzanine.

BRIAN. Let's go.

JEREMY. I am — if you'd just listen — on your bloody side.

He realises he's alone. He takes out his keys, goes to the office. Realises the door is ajar. Pushes it open. He goes in. Drinks in the scene. He sits. In a sudden gesture, he sweeps the paper cups and debris off the desk. Then he unfolds 'The Times', which is open at the letters page. He circles a letter with a pen.

'Dear Sir, I would like to bring to your attention . . . the case of P.M. Lermontov . . .'

He picks up the telephone, dials 0:

Hallo, could you get me Directory —
    I'm sorry?
    The revolution is the festival of *what?*

He puts the phone down. A moment. Then he stands, goes into the corridor as two POLICEMEN *run in.*

POLICEMAN. Ah, professor. Have you seen — ?

JEREMY. Now, chance'd be a fine thing.

Pointing:

Thataway.

Scene Nine

The voice of RICHARD NIXON, *speaking on 30th April, 1970.*

RICHARD NIXON. Tonight, American and South Vietnamese units will attack the headquarters of the entire communist military operation in South Vietnam. This key control centre has been occupied by the North Vietnamese and Vietcong for five years, in blatant violation of Cambodia's neutrality. This is not an invasion of Cambodia.

AMANDA's house. 1st May, 1970. CATHY sits cross-legged on the floor, downstage, wearing stereo headphones, connected to a record player, playing a pile of singles. We cannot hear the music.

Upstage, AMANDA and TEDDY WEINER, CATHY's father. He wears a light overcoat and carries a briefcase. He is fifty-two years old. NIXON's voice comes from the TV news. AMANDA switches it off.

AMANDA. The first of May 1970. First May Day of the new decade. And your president goes mad.

WEINER puts down his case, lays his overcoat over it.

How did you hear?

WEINER. They have a telex at the conference. It's quite a story, after all. His father's a big wheel in oil.

AMANDA. I know.

WEINER looks at AMANDA.

WEINER. 'The second time as farce.'

WEINER goes downstage to CATHY. He pulls up a chair, sits. Hi there.

CATHY pulls off the earphones, looks at him.

CATHY. Oh, Dad. What are you doing here?

WEINER. I've come to share my daughter's grief.

CATHY. You've come to 'share'?

Pause.

WEINER. What can I say?

CATHY looks away.

AMANDA. You could — you could explain, to both of us — 'the second time as farce'.

MARTIN and PHIL come in. They are dressed in vaguely paramilitary gear — MARTIN in bits and pieces of his old school army uniform — a little bruised and battered, but in high good spirits.

MARTIN. Well, have we not had the very merriest of May Days.

PHIL. Have we not indeed.

MARTIN. I should make it clear from the outset that I am
actually a member of the Warwickshire County Cricket Club,
and thus am entirely within my rights to use club premises,
although the rules are mute about doing so at three a.m. in
possession of eight cans of weedkiller. And, indeed, all would
have been quite cool had not the authorities decided to
floodlight the wicket and surround the bloody thing with ten
feet of barbed wire.

He picks up some of the atmosphere.

Good afternoon. I'm sorry, my name's Glass, this is my best
pal Phil, we live here, we have been arrested, beaten up,
we've spent the day in jail, it's not a matter of cosmic
significance, of course, but —

PHIL. Mart.

MARTIN. Um — yes? Hallo? Who is this person, please?

AMANDA. Clark Sullivan was blown up by his own bomb at a
US Air Force Base in Southern California early yesterday.

Slight pause.

And this is Cathy's father.

PHIL. Wow.

WEINER. It's a quotation from Karl Marx. It used to mean a lot
to me. It's a passage about history repeating. Events
occurring, as one might say, twice. First time as tragedy —

AMANDA. The second time as farce. Yes, sure. I know the
reference. That doesn't quite answer my question.

WEINER. OK. You want an answer, you can have one. Of a sort.

Slight pause.

Imagine, if you will, a people. As it happens, mine. Who were
suffering the most terrible and brutal persecutions, and who
one day slipped away. In the early years of this, what was
bound to be the most glorious of all the centuries. And who
came, in dribs and drabs, to the greatest city in the greatest
country in the world, a place where even then the buildings

scraped the sky, and set to work, to earn a future for themselves and for their children.

But, then, quite suddenly, for reasons that at first seemed quite obscure and even arbitrary, their world crashed down around them. And they watched the little they'd created lessen, and then crumble to an ash between their fingers. And perhaps they felt it was their fault, their punishment, for having had such dreams about themselves.

But we, their children, who'd been born in the great city, we didn't feel we were to blame. And some of us, who travelled through the city to its seats of learning, we met older men, who *proved* to us we weren't to blame, and, even more who proved to us who was to blame, and even more who explained to us the reason for the whole of human history, the way it was, the way it is, and how, by the application of man's reason, all of it could change. And if all of that wasn't marvellous enough, they told us, we would be the ones to change it. And we looked before us to the City of the Future, to a light so dazzling and sharp that nothing was distinct but everything was glorious.

But of course there was a price to pay, for the privilege of this exclusive vision, and we were told we'd have to sacrifice our own opinions, our own thoughts, and submit ourselves to orders from above that often seemed odd, confused, and contradictory; and even, sometimes, just plain evil. But we willed ourselves to do it, and indeed there was a pleasure in that exercise of will, there was a passion in the sacrifice, just like the scoring pain of staring into light, which by the very sharpness of its blinding celebrates the fact that if you wanted to, you'd see.

But then, there came a war. And in countries far away from us, but still quite near for our mothers and our fathers, a real sacrifice was being made, whose victims had not chosen it themselves, but had been chosen. And it was cruel and terrible beyond all reason, and our mothers and our fathers, who'd escaped it all those years ago, closed up their eyes, tight shut, and tried not to admit to anybody, least of all themselves, the guilt they felt that they weren't there.

But their children's eyes were open. And we looked back

to the future, to another country, which, if any country was
the future, we had always seen as the very apogee of reason.
And for some the vision was still radiantly bright, opaque
with brilliance. But for others, somehow, in the interim, the
light had faded just enough, for shapes and outlines to
appear, for them to see. And what we thought we glimpsed,
then knew we saw, was corpses.

And if unreason led to piles of corpses, and if reason led
to piles of corpses, too, then where were we to go?

And where we did go was the place that we'd been all the
time, but not been of, the very place our fathers came to all
those years ago. And to our great surprise, we found that we
were welcome in the country of our birth, we were offered
places at its seats of learning, on its journals of distinction, in
its arts. And everything was fine.

Until that is, we realised there was a price to pay for this
as well. And the price was information, on our brothers and
sisters who'd been left behind, still in the cold. And as the
questions were barked out, and answered, as careers were
ruined and lives broken, we closed up our eyes, tight shut,
and tried not to admit to anybody, least of all ourselves, the
guilt we felt that we weren't there.

But then the winds abated, as winds will, and we could
settle down to writing — sometimes, we proposed a mild
reform or two; to administration — sometimes we disposed as
well; and most of all to teaching, values of compassion,
morality and justice, to other people's children and our own.

But then, there came the final, dreadful irony. Our
children, without our blessing or encouragement, decided to
avenge us. And to wield those self-same weapons, of
compassion and morality and justice, against the country
that, they thought, had persecuted and excluded us. But
when they realised that what they were avenging was not our
persecution, but our silence, not our suffering, but our
desperate guilt, they turned those weapons on us.

And they kicked away the ladders we had climbed. And
even spurned the books we'd read to them. And although
there was so much we could remember of ourselves, there
was a kind of madness and unreason in their fury that we

couldn't recognise.

But you were, as you so often pointed out, you were our children.

Directly to CATHY:

And for a while, it was just you. But pretty soon we noticed you'd got company. The company of spoiled brats, from swanky homes, whose families had never known one day of poverty.

To MARTIN:

You see, friend, you discover that the rich are very greedy. It's not enough that they have money and possessions. They want virtue too. They want to feel they're spiritually superior. And to get that feeling in a form that lets you think that everything is someone else's fault, that you are not responsible to anybody or for anything, well, boy, that's truly wonderful.

He finds a piece of paper and scribbles a number. He gives the paper to AMANDA.

Look, that's my number for the week. Try and have her call me there, OK?

He goes.

MARTIN. Please tell me, why does everyone assume —

CATHY. He's right, of course. We blew it, kiddies, literally.

She takes a small tab from the pendant that CLARK *left her.*

But still . . . we made the news today, oh boy.

MARTIN. What's that?

CATHY. What do you think it is?

She takes the tab. She puts on the headphones. She puts on the record player.

PHIL. The error was the weedkiller. We should have trashed the fucking thing. Burn, babies, burn.

He flails out. CATHY *half hums, half sings along with the record she is playing to herself. Meanwhile, upstage a*

*transformation is beginning: red flags wave, red banners
swirl, smoke billows. The roar of railway engines.*

AMANDA. Today is May Day. We must all remember all the
May Days. The Paris Commune and the General Strike. The
Prague Spring and the May events in France. Red Barcelona.
Red Bavaria.

MARTIN. I want to join. I never want to think, or feel, or be,
like that.

AMANDA. We must remember, we must absolutely not forget
the superhuman things that human beings can and have achieve

MARTIN. I want to be a traitor to my class.

AMANDA. You want to join?

MARTIN. This May Day of all May Days.

*AMANDA goes and finds a membership card. Upstage, a
small prisoner detail enters on one side, an MVD OFFICIAL
on the other. The PRISONER is LERMONTOV. The banners
and flags decorate a Moscow railway station. The smoke is
the steam of the engines.*

OFFICIAL. Prisoner detail, halt! Name!

LERMONTOV. Lermontov.

AMANDA gives MARTIN the membership card. He fills it in, as

OFFICIAL. First name and patronymic!

LERMONTOV. Pavel Mikhailovich.

OFFICIAL. Term! Article!

LERMONTOV. Three years. One nine oh one.

OFFICIAL. Don't say that no one warned you, comrade. Happy
May Day.

*The OFFICIAL turns and walks out. The DETAIL remains.
MARTIN hands the card to AMANDA.*

AMANDA. Well? What does it feel like?

MARTIN (*deflated, but smiling*). I have no idea.

CATHY pulls off her headphones.

CATHY. It's May Day. Mayday Mayday.

Act Two

Marxism can effect a dissociation from personal identity very like that experienced by the protagonist in tragic drama. Having entrusted his imagination, his centre of reality, to the historical process, the Marxist revolutionary trains himself to accept a diminished range and validity of private regard. The logic, the emotional authority of the historical, even where it entails destruction and humiliation to his own person, surpasses the claims, the intensity of the self. Doom is accepted, almost acquiesced in, as being part of the historical truth and forward motion in which individual existence anchors its meaning . . .

George Steiner, *Language and Silence,* **1969**

I allowed myself to be forced into the position of feeling guilty not only about my own indecisions, but about the very virtues of love and pity and a passion for personal freedom which had brought me close to Communism. The Communists told me that these feelings were 'bourgeois'. The Communist, having joined the Party, has to castrate himself of the reasons which made him one.

Stephen Spender, *The God that Failed,* **1949**

Whatever the shades of individual attitudes, as a rule the intellectual ex-Communist ceases to oppose capitalism. Often he rallies to its defence, and he brings to this job the lack of scruple, the narrow-mindedness, the disregard for truth, and the intense hatred with which Stalinism has inbred him. He remains a sectarian. He is an inverted Stalinist. He continues to see the world in white and black, but now the colours are differently distributed. As a Communist he saw no difference between Fascists and social democrats. As an anti-Communist, he sees no difference between Nazism and Communism. Once, he accepted the Party's claim to infallibility; now he believes himself to be infallible. Having once been caught by the 'greatest illusion', he is now obsessed by the greatest disillusionment of our time.

Isaac Deutscher, *Heretics and Renegades,* **1955**

ACT TWO

Scene One

Spots tight on PHIL. *He reads from a used stencil.*

PHIL. One.

Karl Marx was wrong. The working class has not become more immiserated and thus more conscious of itself. It has become richer and less conscious of itself. Two.

What has happened is that capitalism has mutated. Mass production has led to an increasing, stultifying, numbing universe of things. A stereo in every fridge. A family saloon in every tumble-dryer. Three.

We begin to grow aware of movement behind PHIL. *Men and women running, and taking up positions.*

This we call the society of the spectacle. The theatre of struggle has thus shifted from the factory to the supermarket. The ideology of consumption is the consumption of ideology. The working class is owned by what it buys. Four.

Behind this system of constraints there lies an increasingly sophisticated state machine of co-option and repression. Five.

The old left is trapped in old ideas. The real revolutionaries in our society are blacks, gays and women, disaffected youth who demand the right not to be forced to work, the so-called mad refusing to accept the 'logic' of an insane world. Six.

Sirens begin to wail. More people moving in behind PHIL.

To unite these groups we must provide examples of the possibility of change. The bullet and the bomb are not the real revolution but they are real metaphors of revolution. Seven.

An action of guerilla warfare serves to show that the power of the state can never be invincible. Such action will destroy this myth, even if we are destroyed ourselves thereby. We are the harbingers of the coming storm. We are the whirlwind.

Suddenly, the stage is flooded with the light of car headlamps. PHIL *is surrounded by armed* POLICEMEN *and* WOMEN, *their handguns aimed directly at him.*
    A DETECTIVE *steps forward.*

So I wrote this?
You are claiming that I duplicated this?
What's wrong with that?

DETECTIVE. Well, for a start, because it's crazy, Phil.

Scene Two

The Hospital Camp in Dubrovlag camp complex in Mordovia, the Soviet Union. Autumn 1971. Evening.
    A row of naked light bulbs. Two PRISONERS, *in grey quilted jackets, sit on a bench in the outer area of a guardhouse. In front of them, on the ground, a stretcher, on which lies a* PRISONER *under a rough blanket.*
    One of the sitting prisoners is a young man called KOROLENKO. *The other is* LERMONTOV.

KOROLENKO. Dubrovlag. Oak Forest Camp. Garden of Eden.

He looks at LERMONTOV, *who says nothing.*

Hey. Adam and Eve. First communists. Know why?

LERMONTOV *looks at* KOROLENKO.

No clothes, one apple between them, and they thought they were in paradise.

KOROLENKO *laughs.* LERMONTOV *a slight smile.*

All right. D'you know what's similar, between the Garden of Eden and the Great Soviet Socialist Democracy?

LERMONTOV. No, tell me.

KOROLENKO. God creates Eve, says to Adam, go on, choose a woman.

LERMONTOV (*smiles, turning away*). Mm.

KOROLENKO. OK. What will Lenin Boulevard be called in twenty years?

LERMONTOV. I've no idea.

KOROLENKO. You're under arrest.

LERMONTOV *laughs*.

So. What you in for?

LERMONTOV. Me? I spoke to the wrong people.

KOROLENKO. Oh, ar? Different with me. I spoke to the right people.

LERMONTOV. What d'you mean?

An OFFICER *enters briskly.* KOROLENKO *leaps to his feet,* LERMONTOV *stands more formally.*

KOROLENKO. Please, sir. Please, Comrade Sir.

OFFICER. Yes, what?

KOROLENKO. Please, Comrade Sir. We need an escort. To take this patient back to the ward, sir.

OFFICER. Patient?

KOROLENKO. Yes, sir. He's had an operation. The anaesthetic will be wearing off.

OFFICER. An operation? Anaesthetic? What d'you think I am? A doctor?

KOROLENKO. No, sir.

OFFICER. Well, then. There you are.

He strides out. KOROLENKO *looks at the* PRISONER *on the stretcher.*

KOROLENKO. Do you think he's waking up?

LERMONTOV. Don't think so.

KOROLENKO. No.

They sit.

Well, it all started, something of a cockup, really. See, I was working in the coalmines, in Donetsk, you know it?

LERMONTOV. Well, I've heard of it.

KOROLENKO. And there were all kinds of problems. Safety regulations weren't being met. Dangerous build-ups of methane gas. And we weren't being paid our proper Sunday bonuses. So a gang of us, well, got together, and refused to work Red Saturdays. And we all got dismissed.

Well, this didn't seem quite fair to me.

So I went to Moscow. They allow you to, three days. And I went to the offices of the Praesidium of the Supreme Soviet. Huge reception rooms. Hundreds of people, milling round. You mill around for hours.

Then finally you see a grey man in a little booth. And he asks you what you've come to say. And so I did.

And after some time, with me telling and him listening, he calls up another man and he takes me off to hospital. And I sa look, I'm fine, I don't feel ill at all. And they say, yes, well, comrade, that's the point.

They said I had 'a mania for struggling for justice'. And I said, well, so did V.I. Lenin. Didn't he? I mean, if it hadn't been for V.I. Lenin, mania-ing away for justice, we'd still have the tsar. Mean, wouldn't we? And so they tell me I am obviously suffering from 'grandiose delusions' too.

They took me home. To a hospital at home. And injected me with sulphur. And I *did* feel ill, then, very ill. And after three or four months, they released me.

But, still, it didn't seem to me to be particularly fair.

So I started writing letters. Well, I wasn't going to go to Moscow, after last time, was I? So I wrote to Comrade Brezhnev, and to Comrade Kosygin, and the Comrade President Podgorny. And to many other comrades. But, apparently, these comrades, these great men, are of a highly nervous and susceptible disposition, because, lo 'n' behold, I gets hauled up in court *again,* accused of causing 'em considerable agitation. And apparently, I found, there is this cunning little law . . .

But I've only three weeks left. And then I'm free. Look on the bright side, eh?

Pause.

So, who d'you talk to, then?

LERMONTOV. I'm sorry?

KOROLENKO. Said, you talked to the wrong people.

LERMONTOV. Yes. I assembled a petition. And I sent the text to *Pravda*. They decided that they didn't have the space to print it, so I gave it to the *New York Times*.

KOROLENKO. Oh, well. They don't take kindly to that kind of thing, now do they?

LERMONTOV. No. There are several cunning little laws.

A WOMAN DOCTOR, in civilian clothes, enters briskly, KOROLENKO leaps up. LERMONTOV follows.

KOROLENKO. Ah, doctor. Comrade Doctor.

The DOCTOR carries on.

Comrade Doctor!

The DOCTOR turns.

DOCTOR. Yes?

KOROLENKO. We are the stretcher party, Comrade Doctor. We need an escort, for this prisoner. To return him to his ward.

Slight pause.

DOCTOR. Am I a doctor?

KOROLENKO. Yes?

DOCTOR. Am I an escort?

KOROLENKO. No?

DOCTOR. Do you need a doctor, or an escort?

KOROLENKO. Well —

The DOCTOR goes quickly out. The PRISONER moves slightly.

He's coming round! He definitely moved!

Silence.

LERMONTOV. What was his operation?

KOROLENKO. Oh, an ironmonger's job.

LERMONTOV. I'm sorry?

KOROLENKO. Kettle spout. Spoon handle. Bits of barbed wire. Stuff like that.

Slight pause.

Not for the first time, either. This one, once swallowed an entire set of dominoes.

He sits. LERMONTOV *sits. Pause.*

You writing in here, then? Things for the West, in here?

LERMONTOV *says nothing.*

I sometimes think, if people only knew . . .

Pause.

LERMONTOV. Then what?

KOROLENKO. It wouldn't happen.

LERMONTOV. No?

Pause.

Look, I have a friend. In Moscow. His name's Leonid Pugachev. And it's a good name, because there is a squat and ugly English dog, a snub-nosed little creature, but with great energy and affection, they call a pug-dog. Well, that is my friend. And he's a university professor: and he has most of what our society can offer; a good job, good apartment, foreign travel, even, sometimes, to the West, to conferences, and symposia . . . And he knows. Of course he know.

KOROLENKO. Think so?

LERMONTOV. And I think also of a writer whom I don't know personally and I doubt if I ever shall. Called C.I. Kaminskaya, who writes articles in *Izvestia.* And who once wrote an article on me. An extraordinary polemic. Misfit, renegade. And my fear is that C.I. Kaminskaya really is the trumpet of this people. That the dumb hatred she expresses really is the general will.

KOROLENKO. Oh, yes?

LERMONTOV. And there is someone else who occupies my mind.

KOROLENKO. Who's that?

LERMONTOV. My friend. Apparently, they say, that somewhere on the further reaches of this wilderness of camps, there is a prisoner who fought at Kronstadt. Who has been here ever since that sailors' rising was put down by Trotsky, fifty years ago. And that old man has seen Utopia's refuse pile up all around him, all those years: all those generations of class enemies, class traitors, ists and iks and ites: adventurists, capitulationists, and Mensheviks and schizophrenics; Trotskyites, Bukharinites and Titoites . . . Until the pile of shit and sewerage, the effluent of paradise, rose up to drown the spires and steeples of the city . . . And through all of them this old man passes, like a ghost, our Holy Fool. And having seen it all, says nothing.

Pause.

KOROLENKO. So you are writing then.

Pause.

Writing things like that down, for the West.

Pause.

I'm out in three weeks, me.

Slight pause.

LERMONTOV. What is your name?

KOROLENKO. I'm Anatoly Korolenko.

LERMONTOV. From Donetsk.

KOROLENKO. That's right. And your name?

LERMONTOV. Pavel Lermontov.

Pause.

How can a human being not trust someone?

KOROLENKO. That's the spirit.

Pause. A CHIEF OFFICER *enters.* KOROLENKO *leaps to his feet.* LERMONTOV *follows, quicker.*

Chief Officer! Chief Comrade Officer! Two prisoners require an escort to transport this prisoner to his ward, Comrade Chief Officer Chief Sir.

Pause.

CHIEF OFFICER. Is this — are you complaining?

KOROLENKO. No, sir!

CHIEF OFFICER. Do you want the cooler?

KOROLENKO. No, sir!

Slight pause.

CHIEF OFFICER. Right.

The CHIEF OFFICER *goes out. The two men remain at attention.*

KOROLENKO. I think you're wrong. I think there's millions out there. Misfits. Sure.

Two clangs — a hammer on a rail. Slight pause. Two more. KOROLENKO *breaks his stance. Outraged:*

And now it's Lights Out. *Lights Out.* We're still *here.*

He throws himself on the bench. The PRISONER *coming round.*

PRISONER. Uh? Wha?

LERMONTOV. My friend. How often must you be betrayed, before you feel despair?

Blackout.

Scene Three

JEREMY CROWTHER's *house in London, February 1972. Darkness — we're in the middle of a power cut.* JEREMY, *now forty-four, appears with a lit candelabra. MARTIN — now twenty-seven — is there too.*

JEREMY. The university gave it to me. I put it round, I already had a watch.

MARTIN. Yes, I think I get one as an heirloom.

Slight pause.

JEREMY. Look, would you like a drink?

MARTIN. No thanks. Unless you've got a bitter lemon, or a —

JEREMY. Well, I'm sure I've something on those lines.

JEREMY goes to the drinks table.

MARTIN. It's my effort at revolutionary discipline.

JEREMY (*pouring drink*). Oh, yes. I see.

Slight pause.

I don't recall you as a person that amenable to discipline.

MARTIN. Well, people change.

He brings over MARTIN's drink.

So, you're in London now?

MARTIN. That's right. Stoke Newington.

JEREMY. Of course. And did you finish your MA?

MARTIN. Uh — no.

JEREMY. I see. So, what —

MARTIN. Oh, I'm doing it full time.

JEREMY. The revolutionary bit.

MARTIN. That's right. I've got this small trust fund, and it seemed the only thing to do.

JEREMY. Rather than give away fivers to the starving in the street?

MARTIN. Indeed.

JEREMY. It being so tricky, nowadays, to find them.

MARTIN. Certainly round here.

JEREMY. Well, it is your money.

MARTIN. Yes, that's what we felt.

JEREMY. Oh, is there a Mrs Glass?

MARTIN. The Party.

The lights come on. JEREMY *lives in a comfortable house, with a distinct country feel.* MARTIN *takes it in during the following.*

JEREMY. Ah, splendid. So. The Party.

MARTIN (*handing* JEREMY *a paper*). Well, it's more 'a group'. Please, do have a paper.

JEREMY. Thank you. Now, you would be — Maoists?

MARTIN. More like, sort of Trots.

JEREMY. What sort?

MARTIN. Well, we don't believe, if Trotsky farted in the spring of 1934, then it stays true for ever and for aye.

JEREMY. Do people think that?

MARTIN. Sure. Had one or two of them ourselves, in fact, until they got chucked out.

JEREMY. I see.

Slight pause.

Yes, I think I saw your leader on the box the other days. James — Grain? He was going on about this bloody coal strike. And dragging in the Londonderry business too, which struck me as, inopportune . . . But tell me, you know the toiling masses so much better than I do, I mean, I'd assumed your average flying picket wouldn't give the time of day to an Irish psychopath, or would he? I merely ask for information.

Pause.

Your cigarette's the wrong way round.

Which it is. MARTIN *reverses it.*

MARTIN. Yes, I think you're right. But, it's remarkable how

fast things move. I mean, who'd have thought a year ago,
eleven thousand engineers, all over Birmingham, would down
tools, march across the city, close down a coke depot, and
win a miners' strike? Who would have believed the poor old
working class, written off by everybody, right and left,
would actually, suddenly, behave like heroes?

JEREMY. Ah, yes, is it not Lennon who reminds us —

MARTIN. And who's to say, in twelve months' time, they
wouldn't do the same to get British imperialism out of
Ireland. I'm sorry. You were saying. Lenin.

JEREMY. Len*non*, actually.

He notes that MARTIN's *glass is still full. He goes to help
himself.*

Forgive me. Whenever I hear the word 'imperialism', I reach
straight for the bottle. John Lennon, isn't it?

MARTIN. What is?

JEREMY. 'A working class hero's something to be'?

He stands, sipping his drink.

Why did you come and see me?

MARTIN. I'm sorry, I don't know what's happened.

JEREMY. Well, you rang up, and you asked me if I'd mind —

MARTIN. I meant, to you.

Pause.

JEREMY. You could say, I was brutally assaulted by the real
world.

MARTIN. I have a friend who was recently, and brutally,
assaulted by the real police.

JEREMY. I'm sorry.

MARTIN. And has just been jailed for ten years.

JEREMY. Good God. Whatever for?

MARTIN. For running off a stencil on his duplicator.

JEREMY. Oh, yes. The bombings trial. They tried to blow up,

what was it? A cottage in the Cotswolds? Belonging to some ludicrously junior Minister of State?

MARTIN. Yes, Hugh Trelawney. Man who wrote the Housing Bill.

Slight pause.

There's an appeal. And a campaign. And that's actually why I came to see you.

Pause.

JEREMY. Oh. Oh, dear.

MARTIN. It being thought, in fact by me, distinguished man of letters, record of support for various progressive causes . . . silly of me.

JEREMY. Well, you really should read other newspapers.

Pause.

I'm sorry. How embarrassing for you. D'you think he's innocent, your friend?

MARTIN. I've really no idea.

JEREMY. I've just stopped being sorry.

MARTIN. Was there a moment? Road to Damascus, sudden burst of light?

JEREMY. No, I don't think so . . . Shall we say, the hyphen linking 'socialist' and 'democratic' stretched and stretched, and eventually snapped.

Slight pause.

For all the usual boring reasons.

MARTIN. Name some.

JEREMY. Oh, must I? They all sound so commonplace and lame . . . Well, I suppose I realised, that you can't reduce the diversity of people to a mathematical equation, that in the end the only way to make men uniform is to put them all in one, that come the crunch there is always what you would doubtless call a fundamental contradiction between the urge to make men equal and the need to keep them free . . .

Which is why idealism, compassion, all those gleaming
impulses, will always, *always* mutate into a kind of sullen,
atavistic envy, which I am now convinced is the worse and
most corrosive of the deadly sins —

MARTIN. You don't think, people are envious as a result of
other people's avarice? Lazy because they're greedy? Angry
because they're proud?

JEREMY. You've left out lust.

MARTIN. Well, I don't believe the revolution's fucking in the
street.

JEREMY. Oh, don't you, any more?
I think, in fact, now you ask me, yes, there was a moment.
A Kronstadt, if you like. It was in October 1969. And there
was a sit-in, or a sleep-in, or a be-in, at the university. And
the issue was — I can't remember, banning something,
somebody recruiting somebody to something, or perhaps a
speaker or a lecturer whose views weren't to their taste . . .
And I thought, oh no. Oh, here we go again. The same mean,
grey, lazy, and, yes, envious distrust of anything that
challenged, anything that didn't *fit*. And I thought, oh, come
on, Jeremy: this isn't what you meant at all.

MARTIN. Well, it may not have been what *you* —

JEREMY. And then I read a letter in *The Times,* from someone
with some unpronounceable East European name, about a
Russian dissident who'd been arrested for the crime of
circulating a petition. A petition, I may say, not concerned
with the right of people to throw bombs at members of the
government, or even dump their garbage in my office, but
about the right to public demonstration, a privilege which in
this country is as you know quite reverently protected.

MARTIN. Do you think it *shouldn't* be quite reverently —

JEREMY. The man was sentenced to three years. For
'discrediting the system'. And then he smuggled out a
statement from the camps, about the camps. And was
sentenced to another seven. For 'agitation to subvert the
state'. And I thought, now, *that's* the type of man that I

admire. I'm with the malcontents and the subversives. I don't think I've changed.

Pause.

MARTIN. Well, I'm naturally very sorry.

JEREMY. Naturally.

MARTIN. But one thing's clear, at least.

JEREMY. What's that?

MARTIN. 'A middle-class hero is something to be.'

JEREMY *doesn't know what to say. He shrugs. He opens* MARTIN's *newspaper. He looks at it. He looks at* MARTIN. MARTIN *moves to get his coat.*

Well, I think I'm going now.

JEREMY. I mean, do tell me, if you actually agree — I'm quoting from your organ — that 'the elitists and the snobs will tell you that the only thing that's worth the name of "culture" is grand opera and boring plays about dead kings and queens. What they forget is that we've got a culture too — even if the posh papers don't take brass bands, pigeon racing and club entertainment seriously. The difference of course is that our culture's actually *fun.*'

MARTIN *looks at him.*

I mean, I merely ask —

MARTIN. For information. Yes. You know what strikes me, Jeremy?

JEREMY. What's that?

MARTIN. That I was wrong.

JEREMY. Well, glory be.

MARTIN. I think, in fact, it wasn't so much that you hadn't been to Spain, but that you weren't a red *at Trinity*. To be quite frank. Sir.

JEREMY. Yes.

Pause.

You know the only thing you've said that gives me any hope at all?

MARTIN. What's that?

JEREMY. That this bomber is your friend.
  Because that means that your love for the whole of humankind has not yet strangled, quite, your capacity to love the people whom you actually know.

MARTIN. That's hope for what?

JEREMY. That you'll get out, before it does.

  Pause.

MARTIN. No need. It won't. There is no contradiction.

  Pause.

JEREMY. No?

  MARTIN *stays on stage as the set changes around him.*

Scene Four

Outside a meeting hall in London, early February 1974. Six PAPER-SELLERS, of either sex, forming a line up to the door of the meeting hall. PEOPLE attending the meeting thus have to run a kind of gauntlet. MARTIN walks towards the door. EVERYONE muffled up against the cold.

1ST PAPER-SELLER. *The Workers' Week!*

2ND PAPER-SELLER. *The Revolutionary Worker!*

3RD PAPER-SELLER. *The Revolutionary Marxist Worker!*

4TH PAPER-SELLER. *Socialist Vanguard!*

5TH PAPER-SELLER. *Morning Star?*

  MARTIN *turns to the* 5TH PAPER-SELLER, *giving the* 6TH PAPER-SELLER *no chance to promote his/her wares.*

MARTIN. No thanks. If I want to do a crossword, then I'll buy *The Times.* Hey, James!

6TH PAPER-SELLER. Um —

He has seen JAMES GRAIN *enter. He hurries over.*

JAMES. Ah, Martin, how —

MARTIN. James, I want to talk to you.

1ST PAPER-SELLER. *The Workers' Week.* Kick out the Tories.

JAMES. *The Worker's Fortnight,* soon, if our print-shop is to be believed.

MARTIN. My article, for the internal bulletin.

JAMES. Yes, what —

MARTIN. It was rejected.

JAMES. Absolutely. It was felt to be politically inopportune.

MARTIN. The *internal* bulletin.

JAMES. Well, exactly.

2ND PAPER-SELLER. *The Revolutionary Worker.* For socialism and a Labour Victory.

JAMES. Make up your mind, I'll buy the paper. (*To* MARTIN.) And 'internal' now means workers, I am glad to say. You know, the people who have shut down British industry two days a week, and are presently engaged —

MARTIN. Did you read it?

JAMES. Yes, of course.

MARTIN. What did it say?

JAMES. Is this a test? It was critical of the Party line, and it contained a number of self-serving distortions of the truth.

MARTIN. Name some.

JAMES. Well, there was the question of the All-Industrial. That did seem to bother you.

MARTIN. It bothered people who were not allowed to put their case.

JAMES. Such as?

MARTIN. The women's caucus.

JAMES. Yes. The conference was, as you know, an attempt to

build a grass-roots workers' faction in the party. The group that you refer to consisted by and large of teachers. One I believed worked part-time in an engineering firm. They were concerned with issues which bore no relation to the subject of the conference.

3RD PAPER-SELLER. *The Revolutionary Marxist Worker.* The paper that supports the miners.

JAMES. Well, you shatter me.

4TH PAPER-SELLER. *Socialist Vanguard?*

MARTIN. Thank you, we subscribe. And there was indeed —

JAMES. And there was indeed the matter of the paper.

MARTIN. Yes.

JAMES. And the Party's policy that it should be accessible to workers.

MARTIN. And the Party's policy to turn it into *Comic Cuts.*

JAMES. Or put another way, the editorial committee's quite correct decision not to publish long and tortuous articles by you about friends of yours in gaol for acts of individual terrorism.

5TH PAPER-SELLER. *The Morning Star?*

JAMES. No, thank you. When I want a recipe, I buy the *Guardian.*

MARTIN. He was — he is a revolutionary.

JAMES. He may think he is a revolutionary. Objectively, he is nothing of the kind. Any more, I am increasingly convinced, than you are. Now, I really think —

6TH PAPER-SELLER. Um —

As MARTIN *grabs* JAMES' *arm and pulls him downstage.*

MARTIN. Look. I won't resign.

JAMES. I rather doubt that there'll be any need.

MARTIN. I beg your pardon?

JAMES. After the left current — left, the PC began to consider its position on the rightward-leaning elements within the Party. Elements like you.

MARTIN. You can't be serious.

JAMES (*suddenly angry*). Martin, it's very simple. There are things you won't give up. You still have this antipathy to working in a group that's led, if just in part, by manual workers. There is something in you that fundamentally distrusts the concept of a leadership, particularly if it's on the surface less articulate than you.

Slight pause.

MARTIN. I stopped. I pulled out the Phil Mandrell thing. I did what I was told.

JAMES. Eventually.

MARTIN. You see, I feel, that there is no contradiction —

JAMES. As I've said before, I couldn't care less what you feel. It's what you think and do. And what your present thoughts are doing is to undermine the seizing of the time through which we are passing at the moment, which is principally defined by the fact that the mineworkers are bringing down the Government.

I'm sorry, Martin, but that's all.

JAMES *quickly upstage and through the door.*

6TH PAPER-SELLER. Um —

MARTIN *following as the lights dim and the setting begins to change:*

Stick-Up? For Brighter Revolutions?

MARTIN *stops.*

MARTIN. Christ. Are you still going?

6TH PAPER-SELLER. Strong.

MARTIN. Then, yes.

Fumbling for change.

Yes, please . . .

AMANDA *enters, as the scene continues to transform into . . .*

Scene Five

AMANDA's *house, February 1974.*

It is a commune in Notting Hill, empty at the moment, except for AMANDA *herself, who carries two glasses and a half-empty half-bottle of scotch.*

AMANDA. So what did you expect?

MARTIN. Well, not a gold watch, I suppose.

AMANDA. I'm sorry?

MARTIN. Look, is that a drink?

AMANDA (*nodding*). Take your coat off and sit down.

She pours a scotch and tosses the bottle on a chair before sitting on its arm. MARTIN *takes off his coat and sits on the arm of another chair.* AMANDA *taps her shoulder.*

Well, here it is.

MARTIN *looks at her and smiles.*

MARTIN. Do you know what struck me? Very forcibly? I've spent four years of patient toil, trying to make SV the Government. And I looked at him, as he put the knife in me, with all the tact and understated charm of Jack the Ripper, and thought: come on, do you really want this man to run the country? James Grain, the man who put the 'rot' in Trotskyism?

AMANDA. And that 'rat' in apparatchik.

MARTIN. Yes.

Slight pause. Clicking:

Oh, yes.

AMANDA. Well, hon, I'm full of sympathy, but if you ask me, you're well out of it. When I left, my feelings were of pure relief. No more, the desperate scramble through the paper, trying to suss out this month's line. No longer, last month, 'smash the Labour Party's stranglehold', and this month, 'build united fronts with social-democratic elements'. In my time, I took up more positions than the Kama Sutra.

MARTIN. You jumped. I was pushed.

Pause. AMANDA *sips her scotch.*

And actually, I rather like the twists and turns. Trying to bend and coil the dialectic, just so far it wouldn't snap.

AMANDA. Well, hon, whatever turns —

MARTIN. And then, today of all days . . . when the working class is actually behaving in a way that it's supposed to, siezing history by the throat, when our fucking rhetoric comes real . . .

Pause.

AMANDA. It's not the end.

Slight pause.

Why should it be the end?

Pause.

Why should it be the only place to be?

Pause.

MARTIN. Well, here you are. In your collective living situation. A pageant of the future, acted out within the very belly of the monster.

AMANDA. Well, we like to think that it's at least a dummy run.

MARTIN. So where's the gang?

AMANDA. There's a squat in Lissom Grove. The pigs gave notice of a bust, and everybody's round there, manning barricades.

MARTIN. And you?

AMANDA. I'm on child-minding duty. Holding coats.

MARTIN. Ah. I see.

Slight pause.

AMANDA. Have you no other shoulder?

MARTIN. Why, do you want me to —

AMANDA. No, no. Just wondered.

MARTIN. Well, there is a she.

Slight pause.

An actress, as it happens, working with a theatre group that calls itself The People's Chemistry. Their present show's called Lock-Out, and in it she plays Mrs Mope, the Daughter, Second Seamstress and the Concept of the Falling Rate of Profit. Her name's Linda Lazonby.

AMANDA. I haven't seen her act.

MARTIN (*enjoying himself now*). Neither have I. She sleeps a lot, though, does that well, which isn't actually bad news, because it means she isn't talking. I mean, politically, you wouldn't classify her as 'advanced'. In fact, she thinks that realpolitik's a Spanish football team, and that the National Front's a meteorological phenomenon.

AMANDA *stands.*

AMANDA. Now, Martin, will you stop that, please.

MARTIN. I'm sorry?

AMANDA. So you should be. Perhaps you ought to —

MARTIN (*slightly blurted*). Look, look, Mand — would you like to go out? For a meal, or something? Talk of old times, weep into our Rogan Gosht?

AMANDA. Martin, I am in charge of three small —

MARTIN. Then tomorrow, when the gang's all back?

Pause.

AMANDA. No, tomorrow there's a tenants' meeting.

MARTIN. Friday?

AMANDA. Women's group.

MARTIN. The weekend?

AMANDA. I would have to check, but I think we're blocking Westway.

MARTIN. Mand. How can I put this.

Slight pause.

Rearrange the following into a well-known phrase or saying . . . Something I've You Always Rotten Fancied.

Pause.

AMANDA. I am tempted to reply, 'Off Fuck'.

MARTIN. Resist it.

AMANDA. Then, quite simply, 'On'.

Slight pause.

MARTIN. 'On'? What? The floor, the sofa? Top of the wardrobe?

AMANDA. 'On' is 'no' spelt backwards.

MARTIN (*going to* AMANDA *and taking her hands*). No, you haven't got the point, it must be actual words, like, um, 'Glass Shouldn't People Stones In Houses Throw'.

AMANDA. *You* haven't got the point. Glass Shouldn't. I should not with Glass.

Pause.

MARTIN. Why not?

AMANDA. All sorts of reasons. Theoretical and practical.

MARTIN. Let's start with practice.

AMANDA. Never on a rebound.

MARTIN. I'm not on a rebound.

AMANDA. No?

Long pause.

MARTIN. The best years of my life.

AMANDA *says nothing.* MARTIN *finds the bottle, and pours himself another scotch. His hands are shaking.*

I tried so hard to please. Did everything that was asked of
me. And willingly I gave. I was offered nothing and I wanted
to be offered nothing. But now — what's left? How could
you do this thing to me?

Pause.

AMANDA. I'm sorry. Know I've always been a good girl. Best
girl. Always done what's wanted, always doing what I'm told.
But still, I'm leaving, with my little suitcase in my hand.
    I'm sorry. Leaving home. Bye bye.

MARTIN *hasn't listened.*

MARTIN. You what? I'm sorry?

AMANDA. Martin, I used to cry —

Suddenly, a group of LIBERTARIANS — *people living in or
connected with the house — burst in. A couple of people are
bleeding. One carries a crying baby. Another is called* RON.

RON. Well, good evening, merry campers. And welcome to the
non-stop Revolutionary Cock-Up Show.

AMANDA. What happened?

People rushing around, looking for things, tending wounds.

1ST LIBERTARIAN. They got the fucking time wrong, didn't
they? When we arrived the bastards were already there.

2ND LIBERTARIAN (*to the crying baby*). Choo choo. Be
quiet, baby.

AMANDA. What, in the house?

RON. All over it. The silly fuckers didn't change the locks. Rule
One. Change all the locks.

2ND LIBERTARIAN. Choo choo.

AMANDA. Where's mother?

2ND LIBERTARIAN. In the pig-pen. She went all hysterical.

3RD LIBERTARIAN. Rule Two. Do Not Go All Hysterical.

The 2ND LIBERTARIAN *takes the baby out. We continue
to hear it cry.*

1ST LIBERTARIAN. Does anybody have the name of our tame bent lawyer?

MARTIN (*to* AMANDA). Was this — a real family?

AMANDA. Yes. It was a real, kosher, working-class and homeless, family.

RON on his way out. He turns back.

RON. Well, if it isn't Martin Glass. The noted Trotskyite.

The hubbub stops. PEOPLE *look at* MARTIN, *who looks round, nervously.*

Does everyone remember? From 'The Trials of Phil Mandrell'? With Comrade Glass, the great consultant? With his *prima facies* and his *nolle prosequis*? And how we had to have a barrister and we hadn't to be naughty in the public gallery, and take things very seriously indeed?

AMANDA. Look, Ron —

RON. Until, that is, The Party tells him Phil Mandrell is objectively a petit-bourgeois individualist. And suddenly, in the middle of a criminal appeal, when he might have been some use, Comrade Glass goes all transparent, and you cannot see him any more.

The 2ND LIBERTARIAN *has reappeared. The baby is still crying.*

MARTIN. That isn't —

RON. And you know what strikes me? That there are certain things that Martin can't or won't give up. Like his deep hostility to working in a group that isn't *led*. Or if it is, is led by everyone. There's something in him, just can't seem to cope with people who are on the surface less informed than him. And I wonder, sometimes, if in fact he's on our side at all.

MARTIN. Please. Please, don't tell me what I think.

RON. Oh, there's nothing wrong with what you think. That's fine. It's what you don't appear to feel.

AMANDA. Leave him alone.

MARTIN. Shouldn't *somebody* do something with that baby?

RON. Why don't you?

AMANDA. Leave Him Alone.

Pause. RON *shrugs, goes out. The others follow.* MARTIN *stands there.*

MARTIN. Thank you.

AMANDA *shrugs. The baby stops crying.*

Red Barcelona.

AMANDA. Pardon?

MARTIN. A kind of code. Me old mate Phil and me.

AMANDA. Go on.

MARTIN. In the beginning, it was just, the communists were saying that the anarchists were wrong. Mistaken. Incorrect.
   Then their mistakes and incorrectitude were 'objectively' in the interests of the fascists.
   Then 'objectively' the anarchists were fascists.
   Then each individual anarchist became an actual, subjective, conscious Nazi.
   Ergo, my dog's a cat.

AMANDA. That isn't quite what Ron —

MARTIN. Does it always have to happen, Mandy?

AMANDA. Not unless we want it to.

The baby starts to cry again.

MARTIN. Why did you used to cry?

Slight pause. AMANDA *decides not to say it as she'd planned.*

AMANDA. Because . . . I once asked Tanny, if she knew what socialism was. She said, oh, yes, of course. It's going to meetings. Funny old life I've given her. And me.

MARTIN. I once —

AMANDA. You know, I could — it would be possible to skip the tenants' group.

The 2ND LIBERTARIAN *appears with the crying baby.*

2ND LIBERTARIAN. Could someone . . . There's no milk. Could someone go . . .

AMANDA (*moving*). Yuh. Sure.

MARTIN. I once caught a cold on a parade ground.

As the scene splits and changes, MARTIN stays holding his glass of whisky.

Scene Six

A country vicarage, Christmas 1974.
   A comfortable but rather empty room. A little Christmas tree. MARTIN stands with his glass of scotch. We hear from offstage, a grossly inadequate rendering of the carol 'Good King Wenceslas'. It stops. Pause. Enter MRS GLASS, MARTIN's mother. MARTIN looks at her.

MRS GLASS. It wasn't carol singers. Just three grubby boys.

MARTIN. Oh? It sounded like —

MRS GLASS. Not proper carol singers.

MARTIN. Did you give them anything?

MRS GLASS. Oh, no. I ask them if they're collecting, for some charity, and if they say 'no', I don't give a thing. I mean, it's actually begging, isn't it?

Pause.

It starts in mid-November. Actually, I blame the parents.

She goes and pours herself a glass of sherry.

Do you want another sherry?

MARTIN. No. I'm drinking scotch.

MRS GLASS. Well, you can help yourself then.

MARTIN does so.

There used to be the proper carol singers. From the church. With horns and bells. And not just carols either. Real wassailing songs. They'd carry lanterns and we'd have them in. It was bliss.

MARTIN (*under his breath*). Oh, Jesus.

Pause.

MRS GLASS. So you've got a proper job now?

MARTIN. Yes, if you can call the *Islington and Hackney Messenger* a proper job.

MRS GLASS. And you've moved.

MARTIN. Into a state of unwed bliss with a single mother. Yes.

MRS GLASS *does not look at him.*

How long do you keep the vicarage?

MRS GLASS. Oh, just till the New Year, actually. It's kind of them, to let me stay for Christmas. It's been ten months, after all.

MARTIN. New vicar moving in?

MRS GLASS. Oh, no. Nice couple. He's a — captain? Or a 'lieutenant', anyway. But she's British. No, the parish shares a vicar now.

Pause.

It's the upkeep, you see, dear. When it's ten pounds for them to step inside the door, just to *look* at the woodwork, or the guttering. It is the upkeep, really.

Pause.

I suppose it doesn't matter now. Last real Christmas that we'll have. I think, don't you? Before the whole thing falls about our ears.

MARTIN. The whole thing whats?

MRS GLASS. Before your unions bring the whole thing crashing down.

MARTIN. Now, mother, you must stop all that. You know it's only wishful thinking. Wanting it so badly won't bring it any closer.

MRS GLASS *looks at* MARTIN. *Pause.*

MRS GLASS. Do you want to come to midnight mass?

MARTIN. I thought you said —

MRS GLASS. Oh, it's here this year. It's on a kind of rota, actually.

MARTIN. Yes, if you like.

MRS GLASS. I do.

Pause.

I was clearing out some rubbish in the attic, actually. I was thinking about other Christmas Eves.

You and your father sledging in the afternoon. In with a shiver, to the smell of wood-smoke. Mince-pies and mulled claret. And at nearly midnight, crunch across the snow.

I found the crib you and your father made. We've lost a wise man and the ox. And Joseph, actually.

MARTIN. Oh, mother, please, do stop.

MRS GLASS. Stop what?

MARTIN. Saying 'actually' in every sentence.

Slight pause.

Sorry.

MRS GLASS. I didn't know I was.

MARTIN. It never was like that.

MRS GLASS. You won't remember.

MARTIN. Yes I do.

Slight pause.

I remember, every year, three gruesome days of attempting to pretend we were a Christmas card. A kind of seance, trying to raise the nineteenth century. Oh, are you out there, jolly red-faced coachman? Oh, can you hear us, Tiny Tim?

But then it was mother's little yearly treat. Playing at mistress of the manor. With her scarves and wellingtons and fucking mulled red wine.

MRS GLASS *looks away.*

What I do remember, coming back from school, on that

grimy, drafty train, was fantasising how I'd shock the pants
off you this year. What I would do or say. To really sear your
mind.

MRS GLASS. I know. He did that too.

Pause.

MARTIN. Who did it too?

MRS GLASS. Your father.

Slight pause.

He would say, when I'd worked at something, obviously, all
day, at baking, sewing something for the parish, he'd remark:
'Of course, the whole thing's nonsense, isn't it? It's all the
silliest pretence, to stop the silliest of people facing up to
what's real in their lives.' And he would say it laughingly and
kindly, but underneath, such scorn.

MARTIN *goes and fills up his drink.*

Your father was a good man. Noble, in his way. He loved his
kind. But not — I think — his kindred. Actually.
    I'm sorry.

MARTIN. Dust.

MRS GLASS. I beg your pardon?

MARTIN. It's a phrase of Trotsky's.

MRS GLASS. Trotsky.

MARTIN. Human dust.

*A long pause. Then MARTIN moves downstage, and the
vicarage fades away behind him.*

Scene Seven

MARTIN *stands there, as we hear the voice of a RADIO
ANNOUNCER, and AMANDA enters to him. She is dressed up,
and carries a bottle wrapped in paper.*

ANNOUNCER. This is the BBC News, today, Thursday the first
of May 1975, and here are the main headlines. May Day

parades have been held in the streets of Saigon, now renamed Ho Chi Minh City, as the new Communist authorities impose severe penalties for looting, prostitution, and 'all decadent cultural activities of the American variety'.

Lights. A private house in North London. A party, at which MARTIN *and* AMANDA *have just arrived.*

MARTIN. Well, this is typical.

AMANDA. What is?

MARTIN. No sounds. This is a party. Where, pray, are the sounds?

AMANDA. There's supposed to be some tapes arriving. Sixties stuff.

MARTIN. They better have the Troggs.

AMANDA. D'you want to get some food?

MARTIN. No, first things first. I never eat on an empty liver.

AMANDA. Fine.

MARTIN *goes off in search of glasses, as* AMANDA *spots* BRIAN, *now in his early thirties, and crosses to him. On his way out,* MARTIN *passes a conversation between a male* SMOKING PARTYGOER *and a female* NON-SMOKING PARTYGOER, *called* MOLLY.

SMOKING PARTYGOER. Well, I can't see how it's a class question.

MOLLY. Well, that's not the point. Though one might point out what the tobacco companies are up to in the Third World.

SMOKING PARTYGOER. I'm not in the Third World. I'm in Muswell Hill.

MARTIN *returns with two beakers of wine. He stops to overhear.*

MOLLY. But the thing I found most interesting was your remark that you smoke at meetings because you're nervous and you're bored.

SMOKING PARTYGOER. Well, I didn't quite —

MOLLY. And it seems to me you're nervous because you're
  working out some devastatingly impressive speech, to impress
  your friends, and you're bored because you never listen to
  what anybody else has got to say. So if it isn't about class,
  then it's absolutely about gender. No?

  She turns and goes. The SMOKING PARTYGOER *is left
  there. He has half an inch of ash, can't see an ashtray. He
  flicks the ash into his jacket pocket.*

MARTIN (*to* BRIAN *and* AMANDA). My God, it's like St
  Crispin's Day back there.

AMANDA. What do you mean?

MARTIN. Revolutionary nostalgia, rampant in the kitchen.
  With reference the victory of the heroic Vietnamese. I kid
  you not, there's people rolling up their trouser-legs and
  showing off the place a police-horse bit their leg in Grosvenor
  Square.

AMANDA. Now, Martin, you remember Brian?

MARTIN. Yes, of course. Are you still in the —

BRIAN. No. In fact, I've joined the Labour Party.

MARTIN. Heavens. Old Bri, sustaining the illusions of the
  working class in the strategy of electoral reformism?

BRIAN. Well, that isn't quite the way I'd put it.

MARTIN. No?

BRIAN. I'd put it as recapturing the party of the working class
  for the principles of democratic socialism.

MARTIN. Which are?

BRIAN. Well . . . the aspirations which were clearly
  demonstrated by the act of bringing down the Tory
  Government.

MARTIN. But you don't think that in fact the fundamental role
  of social-democratic parties like the Labour Party has been
  precisely to prevent the working class from the achievement
  of those aspirations, by deviating their mass action down the
  channels of . . .

Pause.

The channels of —

BRIAN (*to* AMANDA). Um?

MARTIN. Sorry, it's completely gone.

BRIAN. What's gone?

MARTIN. I can't remember what comes next. No matter. Bound to come back to me.

He smiles. His glass is empty.

I think I'm going to try and liberate our bottle.

He goes.

BRIAN. What's with —

AMANDA. Excuse me, please.

She catches MARTIN up.

Martin, what's wrong?

MARTIN. There's nothing wrong.

AMANDA. That is palpably not true.

He looks at her. She changes tack, puts her arms round his neck.

Lovey, it's happened lots of time before. The stage of history is littered with people who have passed the age of thirty, doing the most wonderfully exciting things. I can think of literally dozens of examples.

MARTIN. No, it isn't that.

AMANDA. What is it, then?

MARTIN. It's nothing.

He takes her arms away, turns and goes. She returns to BRIAN.

AMANDA. I'm sorry. It's our thirtieth tomorrow, and we're taking the whole thing very badly.

BRIAN. Are you two — I didn't think, in Birmingham . . .

AMANDA. No, a recentish development. Oh, hell the what, say I.

BRIAN. Beg pardon?

JAMES GRAIN comes to AMANDA.

JAMES. Amanda.

AMANDA. James.

MARTIN has re-entered with a bottle of wine. He is smoking. He stumbles slightly, nearly into MOLLY, who is engaged in conversation with a small knot of people.

MARTIN. Excuse me. Sorry.

MOLLY. Please, don't smoke that thing at me.

MARTIN passes, but turns back.

MARTIN. Uh — 'plead you to me, fair dame?'

MOLLY. Fuck off.

MARTIN. You what?

MOLLY (*turning back to her conversation*). You heard.

MARTIN to JAMES, AMANDA and BRIAN as:

JAMES (*raising his glass*). Well. Victory.

MARTIN. Who is that woman?

AMANDA. Which one?

MARTIN (*gestures to MOLLY*). That one.

AMANDA. She's called Molly something. Wages for Housework, I believe.

MARTIN. Wages for *what?*

Slight pause.

AMANDA. Wages for Housework. It's a group —

MARTIN. That's what I thought you said.

Slight pause.

JAMES. So, Martin, how's the bourgeois press?

MOLLY is passing.

MARTIN. You know, if you think about it, what has really liberated women is the invention of the vacuum-cleaner, the tumble-dryer and the fridge. Well, I think so.

MOLLY *stops, listening.*

AMANDA (*quietly*). Martin, I'm not sure that I'm presently that interested in what you think.

MARTIN. You see, I feel the problem does come down —

AMANDA (*quietly*). Or what you feel.

MARTIN. I mean, assuming that that slogan is, despite its self-evident absurdity, a serious and practical demand —

AMANDA. I am increasingly convinced, in fact, despite my better judgement, that the problem does come down to what you are.

Pause.

MARTIN. I'm sorry?

Slight pause.

What d'you mean, 'to what I am'?

AMANDA. Martin, do something for me. Please. Stop talking for five minutes and consider, really try to imagine what life would be like if you didn't have a cock. I think that would be really helpful. Actually.

Pause. MOLLY *laughs. She goes off.* MARTIN *and* AMANDA *look each other in the eye.*

MARTIN. Everywhere I turn.

AMANDA. 'What Do You Mean?'

Pause.

BRIAN. Yuh, well, I think that basically the left has underestimated the —

MARTIN. Well. James. Now, is the rumour true, your paper is accusing the Vietnamese of selling out *already?*

JAMES. No, I don't think so.

MARTIN. No? There was excited comment in the drinks queue,

on how many Trotskyists were bumped off by Ho Chi Minh.

JAMES. Well, that's certainly the case.

MARTIN. So what's your prediction, then, for revolutionary Vietnam? Another Stalinist degeneration?

JAMES. Well, I wouldn't be surprised.

MARTIN. Not 'Peace in Vietnam' but 'Victory'?

Slight pause.

JAMES. Martin, what follows is at primer level, suitable for six years and below. We supported Ho Chi Minh because that Stalinist and, as you point out, murderer, was the only person, led the only party, which could win the war.

MARTIN. 'Objectively'?

JAMES. Correct. In the same way as we unconditionally support —

MARTIN. I think in five years time we will all cringe at the memory of tonight.

Pause. A few people have heard this. The buzz of conversation dying, as:

At least, I hope so. Cringe and blush and fidget. Try to change the subject. Hope we will.

Almost EVERYONE *now listening. The odd laugh, as if it's a joke:*

When this one goes all wrong too. And the walls are built and the barbed wire is in place and our dear old rolly-moley midwife has brought forth another bug-eyed basilisk, I hope we'll cringe. Don't you?

Silence.

JAMES. Oh, dear.

MARTIN. But I doubt it. What I imagine will occur is another alibi, like the last time, and the time before, the ravages of civil war, you can't build socialism in one country, oh, if only Stalin hadn't packed the Politburo in 1924 . . . And as once again the proofs pile up that we are catastrophically wrong, we change the question. Or indeed, having predicted that the world will definitely end on Tuesday, we spend Wednesday morning arguing that all this proves is that the apocalypse is bound to roll along by the weekend. That all the stillbirths, all the monstrous misbegottens with no legs or stomachs but with all those twitching ears and beady little eyes, that they're the deviation, and that *therefore* somewhere in the future there must be a norm.

You see, I just no longer can believe, that a third of humankind is living in an aberration. Any more than I believe the workers of the West are straining at the leash to bite their way to communism, if only we could crack the chains that bind them to their masters. I can't understand this crazy nightmare world we've fashioned for ourselves, where devilish social-democrats conspire to muzzle discontent by day, and dastardly reformists plot to deviate the proletariat by night . . .

Whereas it might be possible, might just be possible, that the putative tin soldiers in our class-war game have seen the future, and they don't believe us when we say this isn't what we meant at all . . .

You see, I don't think it's just Stalin, or even Lenin. I think it is the whole idea. That our childlike sense of justice and compassion and fairplay, the thing that got us here, that we must hone and beat it down, from a ploughshare to a sword; that there's no morality except the interests of the revolution, that to be a communist you must purge yourself of the instincts and beliefs that made you one.

And what it leaves us like. We're right and everybody else is wrong, and so we're arrogant; and the fewer of us that there are, the more insufferable we become. But paradoxically, too, we want the world to listen, and they won't, and so we're mean. And the compound, I think, is this terrible unfocussed fury that we seem to nurture in ourselves, that burns us up, and which we beam about us like a blowtorch, branding everything we touch or see.

And what's it all for, in the end? What is it we're disguising when we say, Marx doesn't give a blueprint, we don't know, the process of the struggle will throw up the forms, etcetera . . .

It's a Golden Age. The dialectical return, to some primitive, communal, blissful — something. A Great Leap Backwards, to the childhood of humanity. It's nowhere.

And, for the sake of that, I don't believe, I can't believe, I actually refuse to be required by anybody to believe, that anyone is human dust.

Pause.

They say that every generation has its Kronstadt. Well, today is mine.

Pause.

I feel a great deal better.

MARTIN *goes quickly to the exit. He bumps into the entering* RON. *There is a beat between them. Then* MARTIN *goes out.*

JAMES (*to* AMANDA). I'm sorry.

AMANDA. Well, I suppose . . . it's only rock and roll.

RON. Uh — evening, comrades.

Um . . . Met a young person on the doorstep. Her Renault Five had broken down on the North Circular. She's covered in apology. She's brought the sounds.

Rock music from off.

JAMES. And there they are.

BRIAN (*to* AMANDA). Do you want to dance?

AMANDA. No, I don't think so. Thank you very much.

BRIAN. They better have 'A Whiter Shade of Pale'.

Scene Eight

Frankfurt Airport. Late 1978. Bare stage.
An OFFICIAL *quickly leads in* PAVEL LERMONTOV, *followed by a large gaggle of* REPORTERS *and* CAMERAMEN.
The REPORTERS *shriek questions in several languages.*

The CAMERAMEN *flash away.*

LERMONTOV *looks totally bewildered, as the* OFFICIAL *leads him into a space where a microphone is set up, waiting. All this very fast:*

PRESS (*variously, and in various languages*). When were you released, Mr Lermontov?

>   When did they tell you?
>   Please look over here, Mr Lermontov.
>   What does it feel like, to be in the West?
>   How long ago did you know?
>   Mr Lermontov, just turn your head, please —
>   What do you feel about being exchanged for a Russian spy?
>   Did they tell you in advance?
>   Did you want to be exiled to the West?
>   Just look this way, Mr Lermontov —
>   Do you have any family left in Russia?
>   When are you flying to England, Mr Lermontov?
>   Which hotel are you staying at?
>   How long will you be staying there?
>   How long are you going to stay in England?
>   Do you have any immediate plans?

They are now at the microphone. The jabber goes on, as the OFFICIAL *tries to get silence.*

OFFICIAL. Please, please, ladies and gentlemen —

PRESS. Why did you choose to come to Frankfurt?

>   Here, please, Mr Lermontov —
>   Did you have any idea before today?

OFFICIAL. Please, ladies and gentlemen.

The jabber subsides.

Mr Lermontov.

Pause.

LERMONTOV. Well. Well.

Pause.

Look, um, I — Look.

Slight pause.

There is, a saying in our country. That it seems foolish to spend so much time, as we do, learning to speak, when one . . . When one is not allowed subsequently to do so.

Slight pause.

Now I can speak.

Slight pause.

Now I am free to say what I like.

Slight pause.

I find . . . I have no words to say.

Slight pause.

You will forgive me.

He leaves the microphone. Before the jabber can restart, we see MIKLOS PALOCZI, *now forty-three years old.*

PALOCZI. Pavel.

LERMONTOV (*confused*). I'm sorry —

PALOCZI. Pavel. Miklos Paloczi.

LERMONTOV *doesn't remember.*

Hungary.

LERMONTOV *remembers.*

LERMONTOV. Oh, no. Oh, no.

LERMONTOV *embraces* PALOCZI. *He is crying.*

Oh, no . . .

And the flashbulbs flash around them.

Act Three

If one were to probe into the hearts of many potential and actual Tory supporters — and others besides — one might discover that what worries them most about contemporary Britain was not so much the lack of freedom as its excessive abundance; not so much the threat of dictatorship as the reality of something unpleasantly close to chaos . . . and for Mrs Thatcher to tell a party indignant at the collapse of all forms of authority, and longing for the smack of Firm Government, that the country is suffering from a lack of liberty makes her seem out of touch with reality . . .

Peregrine Worsthorne, in *Conservative Essays*, **1978**

The defence of individual rights has reached such an extreme that society itself is becoming defenceless against certain individuals. And in the West it is high time to defend, not so much the rights of individuals, as their duties.

Alexander Solzhenitsyn, *Harvard Speech*, **1978**

ACT THREE

Scene One

Autumn 1978. A public place. MARTIN *and* JEREMY *meet. They look at each other.*

JEREMY. Three years ago.

MARTIN. That's right.

JEREMY. So long.

MARTIN. I wanted to be sure.
    It does take time. You must remember that. You shove two fingers up the dialectic, bound to get a shock.

JEREMY. Indeed. But, now . . .

MARTIN. What, now?

JEREMY. You're sure?

MARTIN *takes a piece of paper from his pocket. He reads.*

MARTIN. 'The red blood splatters both the
        cities and the plains of the
        beloved fatherland
    The sublime blood of the workers and
        the peasants, revolutionary fighters
        of both sexes . . .
    That red blood liberates us all from
        tyranny.'

Etcetera, etcetera.

He puts the paper away.

The anthem of the Khymer Rouge.

Slight pause.

Oh, absolutely sure.

JEREMY. Then — welcome.

JEREMY *puts out his hand to* MARTIN, *who takes it. Lights fade. In the darkness,* MARTIN's *voice:*

MARTIN (*voice over*). And I looked from face to face, from 'Trotskyist' to 'Libertarian' to 'Democratic Socialist', and I realised that all these faces, from the harshest to the most benign, were set like flint against the way that human beings really are.

Scene Two

During MARTIN's *speech, a spot fades up on* JAMES GRAIN, *reading a copy of 'The Times'. Then, general lights. We are on the far edge of an anti-racist rally-cum-rock-festival, in an open public place, in the autumn of 1978. Upstage, a few people, watching the concert that is taking place further upstage. A few people holding lollipop shaped placards, with slogans in the red and yellow of the Anti-Nazi League. Similarly coloured balloons as well.* AMANDA *comes downstage. She wears a steward's armband.*

AMANDA. Well, James.

JAMES. Amanda. Hallo.

AMANDA. Now isn't this delightful?

JAMES. Isn't it. Have you seen this?

He waves the paper.

AMANDA. Yes. Yes of course I have.

Pause.

Well, as they say —

JAMES. Some fashionable words. We'll hear a lot of them today, I'm sure. The ra-ra words of the bright new ra-ra left. 'Open'. 'Tolerant'. And 'pluralistic'.

AMANDA. Well, yes —

JAMES. Tolerant of *him?*

AMANDA. I rather doubt if he'll turn up. Too busy
supergrassing on his past.

JAMES. Of people who in five years time will be doing the same
thing?

Pause.

AMANDA. You know, I once attempted, unsuccessfully, to tell
Comrade Glass a little about being me.

JAMES. Well, yes —

AMANDA. I tried to tell him how I used to cry. Me and my
child, our noses pressed against the lighted windows,
watching the 2.4 kids playing round the Christmas tree.

Why me? Why couldn't *I* accept things as they were? Why
did *I* have to feel it was all wrong, and that I was put into the
world to set it right?

Well, you know as well as I do. All those opportunities,
those bold bright schools and gleaming universities. That our
folks had never had themselves, but had been through a
slump and then a war to win for us. And if we didn't finish
it, if we didn't get it right, this time, if we didn't actually
complete the building of the New Jerusalem, for them, for
us, then what the fuck were we about?

And I left your party when I realised the one absolute
condition of my membership was checking in those feelings
at the door.

JAMES *is about to reply when* JUDY *strides down from the
upstage group, bearing a clipboard, and also wearing a
steward's armband.*

JUDY. Ah, Mandy.

AMANDA. Jude.

JUDY. The International Brigade.

Slight pause.

AMANDA. I'm sorry?

JUDY. Where are they?

AMANDA. Barcelo — ?

JUDY. The Band. They are on next and not here.

Slight pause.

AMANDA. Well, I'm very sorry, Judy, but —

And BRIAN *has also come in, harrassed, carrying a sensible toy.*

BRIAN. Judy. There is a minor riot in the creche —

JUDY *bangs her forehead with the flat of her hand.*

JUDY. I try to combat bourgeois cultural hegemony.

She strides off.

JAMES. You know . . .

Something in his tone makes AMANDA *and* BRIAN *turn to him.*

There is a moment, and it's not a pleasant one, when you do begin to realise . . .

Slight pause. He changes tack.

There is shortly going to be a General Election. And in our view the Conservatives will win. They will win in part because the working class has been betrayed, not least by those whom we have always said were really on the other side, and who now appear, in their true colours, so to be.

Pause.

The moment, is the moment when you realise that what you've always said is true. When the enemy looks like the enemy. The moment when your rhetoric comes real.

He looks at them a moment, then tosses 'The Times' to AMANDA *and goes out.*

BRIAN. He's got problems with the crossword?

AMANDA. No. Revenge.

BRIAN. I'm sorry?

AMANDA. Old mate Martin. Taking his revenge.

A YOUNG MAN *has appeared. He wears a hideously ripped and pinned Mao jacket, and tiny rectangular glasses with white rims. His hair consists largely of spikes. He carries a guitar case.*

YOUNG MAN. Uh — scuse —

AMANDA *and* BRIAN *look at him and then at each other.*

BRIAN. For me, it all went off with Elton John.

Scene Three

December 1978.
    A suite in a hotel in Kensington. Hightech, tubular design. We are in the sitting-room part. MARTIN *sits making notes on a pad.* JEREMY *is reading newspapers.* MIKLOS PALOCZI *is on the telephone.*

JEREMY (*reading from a newspaper*). The University of Loughborough is planning to spend £20,000 researching something they describe as 'pinball art'.

PALOCZI. That's Andreyushkin? Why not Griboyedov?
    Well, I'll have to speak to him about it.
    Yes, that's right, Paloczi.

He puts the phone down. It rings immediately. He picks it up.

Hallo?

JEREMY. There is a body called 'The Free Media Campaign', which is presently 'demanding' that the NUJ expel from membership all journalists whose work 'uncritically promotes ideas of racial, class or sexual superiority'.

PALOCZI. No I'm afraid that Mr Lermontov is already booked for interview.
    The *Sunday Times*. Today.
    That's right. Exclusively.

He puts the phone down. It rings.

Hallo?

JEREMY. And apparently, it's been proposed that the Inner London Education Authority provide free creche facilities for schoolgirl mothers.

PALOCZI. What, actually in the lobby?

JEREMY. Free in the sense of 'on the rates', of course.

PALOCZI. No, they must ring. Please tell them, they must telephone.

JEREMY. The idea is being given serious consideration.

PALOCZI. And now, please hold all calls.

He puts the phone down as PAVEL LERMONTOV *enters. He looks well brushed and scrubbed, in new clothes.*

JEREMY. Sometimes I think they print these things, deliberately, just to outrage me.

LERMONTOV. Hallo.

PALOCZI. Pavel.

MARTIN *and* JEREMY *to their feet.*
    A note: Although LERMONTOV's *English is good, when he and* PALOCZI *speak alone, we assume they are speaking Russian. There are also moments in conversations with other people when* LERMONTOV *will slip into Russian: usually, as later in this scene, when he cannot remember an English word. So, when he is groping for the word 'blur' later on, the words 'dimness, hazy, foggy' are, as it were, the Russian words for blur, rather than English synonyms. It is important for later events that this device is established in the scene.*

LERMONTOV. Now, these are —

PALOCZI. Now, Pavel, meet —

LERMONTOV. Mr Crowther?

JEREMY. Jeremy.

LERMONTOV. And —

MARTIN. Martin.

PALOCZI. Glass.

JEREMY. Look, I can't tell you how delighted —

MARTIN. I'm terrifically pleased to —

LERMONTOV. There's a man out there. A man, out in the
  street. I've been watching him for half an hour.

  PALOCZI *a quick move towards the other room.*

  He is selling newspapers.

  PALOCZI *turns back to the smiling* LERMONTOV.

  All different shapes and sizes, and of all complexions too,
  I'm sure: left ones and right ones, clever ones and stupid
  ones, serious and trivial — and he seems as pleased to sell one
  as the other. Pleased to please. Like a card-sharper, with his
  papers and his change. A real entertainer. They say that we,
  we 'dissidents', see the West as our hero. Well. I think I have
  found mine.
      Were all those calls for me?

PALOCZI. Yes. Do you want to hear about them?

LERMONTOV (*sits*). Please. It's such a novelty.

PALOCZI (*reading from his notebook*). Well, there's a group,
  based at the London School of Economics, campaigning
  against psychiatric torture. They want you to address them.
  I said yes.

LERMONTOV. Good, good.

PALOCZI. Then the BBC World Service people rang. They want
  you for an interview. They tried to fob us off with a man
  called Andreyushkin, but I told them where they could put
  that. They're calling back.

MARTIN. What's wrong with Andreyushkin?

PALOCZI. Soft. In the section, he is called 'Kerensky'.

LERMONTOV. Ah.

PALOCZI. And then there were lots of papers, but I said the
  Sunday Times . . . And various cranks and crazies whom you
  needn't bother with.

LERMONTOV. I'm sorry, cranks and crazies?

PALOCZI. Well, you know, the type —

LERMONTOV. No, I'm sorry, I don't know.

PALOCZI. Well, like —

Slight pause.

Pavel. There are in Britain, groups, campaigns, committees, with high-sounding titles, all for freedom, liberation, civil rights — but which, if they actually achieved any real influence or power, would put you in a camp again.

LERMONTOV. I see.

Slight pause.

Well, now. Miklos informs me you are taking me to lunch.

JEREMY. Indeed we are.

LERMONTOV. And interviewing me.

MARTIN. That's right.

LERMONTOV. The *Sunday Times.*

PALOCZI. Correct.

LERMONTOV (*to* MARTIN). And you, a former Trotskyite? Is that unusual?

PALOCZI. Um, well —

MARTIN. We tended to prefer 'Trotskyist'.

LERMONTOV. And now? What type of 'ite' or 'ist' are you?

Slight pause.

MARTIN. Well, in fact I find most 'isms' pretty hard to —

LERMONTOV. Oh, come on. Please, tell me. I am interested. After all, I too am, what you might call, a defector.

Slight pause. MARTIN *looks to* JEREMY *for confirmation, and gets it.*

MARTIN. Well, in a sentence, I suppose I realised that men and women are only equal in the prison or the graveyard.

LERMONTOV. Yes?

MARTIN. And that — that all attempts to force them to be equal, every increase in the power of monopoly, the closed shop and the state, lead ultimately to the concentration camp.

LERMONTOV *still looking questioningly at him.*

And that the only social value which means anything is the right of individuals to forge their destinies, uncoerced and undirected, as they will.

PALOCZI. Ah, but do you think they really want it? Freedom?

MARTIN. Who?

PALOCZI. You see, I sense complete contentment. The nation sitting on its quango, with one hand held out for its girocheque, the other filling in its VAT return.

MARTIN. Content?

PALOCZI. Now, freedom *from* is one thing, freedom from want and hunger and disease, they'll vote for that . . . But those who believe that human rights don't *end* with breakfast, those who believe in freedom *for* . . . A small minority. The merest speck.

MARTIN *looks to* JEREMY, *then back to* PALOCZI.

JEREMY. Yes, you know the thing that I can't understand?

MARTIN. What's that?

JEREMY. How it was possible for us to think that if you opened up the sluice-gates, then the lower water automatically bubbles to the level of the higher. Genuinely thought, a couple of good education acts, a few bright modern city libraries, and within a three-month sturdy sons of toil will all be reading Thomas Mann amd whistling Dvorak. Whereas, what actually happened was, a kind of rising silt. Of bingo, dogs, and, pinball. Hardly need 'The Revolution' any more. This is how the world ends, actually: not with a big bang, but a whippet.

MARTIN. You don't think that's unnecessarily pessimistic? You see, I think, that if you really set the people free, if you really broke the shackles of the state, you'd be amazed how many flowers would bloom.

PALOCZI. You think so? Really?

LERMONTOV. What is a whippet, please?

Slight pause.

MARTIN. It's a kind of dog. I'm sorry —

LERMONTOV. What, like a pug?

PALOCZI. No, nothing like a pug.

The phone rings.

And I did say no calls.

LERMONTOV, *who is nearest, answers the telephone.*

LERMONTOV. Hallo?
    Yes, yes, hallo?

He hands the phone to PALOCZI.

You had better take it. It is apparently a man of some importance. Hence, his getting through.

PALOCZI. Yes, who is this?
    Oh, I'm sorry. Yes. Hallo.

LERMONTOV. It's very odd.

PALOCZI. Yes, that was him.

LERMONTOV. We used to talk in English, in the camps, because of course the guards were not well educated, and they couldn't understand us.

PALOCZI. Well, yes, sometime next week?

LERMONTOV. But now I'm here, surrounded by it, and it's just a — (*To* PALOCZI.) Dimness, hazy, foggy?

PALOCZI. Yes, absolutely. Both of them.

He puts the phone down. LERMONTOV:

That's 'Just a blur'.

LERMONTOV. A Blur.

PALOCZI. There is a body, called the Committee in Defence of

Liberty. They want to give you an award. Big dinner, and you make a speech. That was the chairman. He's a former member of the Government, now a Provost of a Cambridge College. He wants to invite you there. To meet him. Have a chat. Discuss the matter.

LERMONTOV. An award?

PALOCZI. You know, a statuette, or something.

LERMONTOV. And 'liberty' means freedom?

PALOCZI. Yes.

Slight pause.

LERMONTOV. Then, of course. I'd be most privileged.

Slight pause.

And now, to lunch?

PALOCZI. To lunch!

He claps his hands. Bustle. They go out. MARTIN *lingering.* PALOCZI *and* LERMONTOV *have gone.*

MARTIN. Look, Jeremy.

JEREMY. Yes, what?

MARTIN. Who is that man?

JEREMY. Miklos Paloczi. Writes for the Economist.

MARTIN. I mean, *who* is he? What's he doing?

JEREMY. Well, what he's done is to spend eight years campaigning for our friend to be —

MARTIN. I mean, what is he doing now?

Slight pause.

JEREMY. Look, Martin. The man does have impeccable credentials. In fact you could say, that unlike me, he left Hungary, over the Party.
Now, shouldn't we —

MARTIN. And 'The Committee in Defence of Liberty'?

JEREMY. It's a pressure group. As its name implies. I think I'm on its council.

MARTIN. And this Provost?

JEREMY. Is a man called Hugh Trelawney. Martin —

MARTIN. Hugh Trelawney.

PALOCZI *has re-entered to find out the reason for the delay.*

PALOCZI. A tragic story, in a way. Poor bloke got kicked upstairs. There was some, well, unpleasantness, surrounding the enactment of his Housing Bill.

MARTIN. I know.

PALOCZI. But I think you'll find, an interesting man.

MARTIN. I'll find?

PALOCZI. Well, I hope you're coming too.

Scene Four

The Provost's rooms, a Cambridge College, January 1979.

An upstage and downstage area, divided — we imagine — by doors or a curtain. The downstage area, with a roaring fire, and comfortable chairs, is presently empty. Upstage, LERMONTOV is being introduced to a group of well-wishers, dons, undergraduates and others by PALOCZI. JEREMY is there too, as is MARTIN, who is in the downstage area, looking for an ashtray. JEREMY nods to the College Provost, HUGH TRELAWNEY, and the two men come into the downstage area.

TRELAWNEY. Now, Mr Glass?

MARTIN. That's right.

JEREMY. Martin, meet Hugh Trelawney.

MARTIN. How do you do?

TRELAWNEY. Delighted you could make it. Filthy weather.

MARTIN. Not at all.

Slight pause.

TRELAWNEY. Have you been to Simeon before?

MARTIN. No, I haven't.

TRELAWNEY. We are very proud of —

MARTIN. It is most agreeable.

Slight pause.

TRELAWNEY. I read with interest your piece on Lermontov, where was it?

MARTIN. *Sunday Times.*

TRELAWNEY. Great interest. As with your pieces on your own, trajectory, the series in — the *Standard?*

MARTIN. No, the daily *Times.*

TRELAWNEY. Indeed.

Slight pause.

JEREMY. Um, Martin. Hugh was saying —

TRELAWNEY. Hugh will say.

He gestures MARTIN *to sit.* MARTIN *perches on the edge of a sofa.*

In fact, Hugh thought of offering you a job.

MARTIN. What kind of job?

TRELAWNEY. Our little, group, requires a full time officer.

MARTIN. To do —

TRELAWNEY. We had in mind, the preparation of a kind of, manifesto.

MARTIN. For?

TRELAWNEY. To outline what, in our view, the priorities of the next Goverment should be.

Slight pause.

That is assuming, naturally —

MARTIN. Of course. I'd need to know, precisely, where you —

TRELAWNEY. As would we.

Pause.

MARTIN. You first?

TRELAWNEY. Well, where to start?

> TRELAWNEY *smiles. A slight nod to* JEREMY, *who withdraws a little upstage, and sits. We begin to lose a sense of the upstage area.*

> It's an outworn phrase, of course, but the next election will, in my view, be the most important since the war. The showdown, if you like. The polity a pyramid, the electorate a silver ball, perched on the top, unsteady, could roll either way.

MARTIN. A pyramid has several sides.

TRELAWNEY. Of course. And the side that you are on — the side that you are *now* on — is very clear. Unless we want to end up in the Gulag, stop the clicking ratchet of the state.

MARTIN. That's right.

TRELAWNEY. Health warnings off the packets, nanny off our backs. Free, adult men and women in a free, grown-up society.

MARTIN. Correct.

TRELAWNEY. And if people want to buy pornography or drugs, and if they're offered on the market at a price they are prepared to pay, then nobody, and least of all the state, should interfere.

MARTIN. I'm glad that you agree.

TRELAWNEY. I think — about your article — the word I used was 'interesting'.

> *Pause.*

MARTIN. Go on.

TRELAWNEY. Well, the fact is, on a cursory inspection of your output, I have noticed that the word 'right' — as in 'human right' — has graced your columns, oh, a hundred times. But I've only seen the word 'duty' once. In a sentence starting, 'In the free world, we have a duty to . . .', protect our threatened liberties, or something of that ilk.

MARTIN. What's wrong with human rights?

TRELAWNEY. That so often they're not balanced by a corresponding consciousness of obligation.

MARTIN. You tug my forelock, I'll tug yours?

TRELAWNEY. Well, if you like.

MARTIN. I see.

TRELAWNEY. I'm not convinced that's so.

Slight pause.

My Party has an interesting history. In the nineteenth century, the age of liberalism, it stood for land, tradition, church and state, against the rising tide of *laissez-faire*. Against the collapse of ancient hierarchies, and indeed the obligations that went with them, kindness, charity: against, in short, the cold and calculating face of commerce.

MARTIN. And the liberties that went with *that*.

TRELAWNEY. Indeed. Whereas, in our own century, things changed. Because the enemy had changed. Now it was socialism. Grey, monolithic, smothering. As you say, the Nanny State. Her charges guarded against every challenge, from the cradle to the grave. Her nursery the council house, her schoolroom a closed shop. Her motto, 'I want always gets'. And against *that*, we stood up for enterprise, for the brisk, chill wind of competition, for individual liberty. And there are, in the Party, many, like yourself, who think that battle is still on.

MARTIN. You don't?

TRELAWNEY. I think it's won. I think that socialism, as a reputable intellectual concept, is quite dead. A 'wasm' in our times.

MARTIN. Well, honestly, you could have fooled —

TRELAWNEY. In the form of state control of the means of production, distribution and exchange.

MARTIN. There is another form?

TRELAWNEY. Well, more a residue. A kind of putrefaction, left there, breeding in the body politic. Which it is now our party's task to purge.

MARTIN. I see. And so, what antidote do you prescribe?

TRELAWNEY. Well, in a word: Authority.

Pause.

MARTIN. Well, I'm sorry, Mr Trelawney. But I think I've spent quite long enough believing that the choir of humankind sounds best in unison. I'm really very sorry.

TRELAWNEY. Not unison — so much as harmony.

MARTIN *is about to say something, but* TRELAWNEY *goes straight on.*

Look, I do — I think I understand. How hard it is.

MARTIN. How hard what is?

TRELAWNEY. What you have had to do. Remake your life. Both for you and Lermontov. You have both been through the centre of the fire. You've both been branded by the century.

MARTIN. Him just a little more than me.

TRELAWNEY. Which is why you are both such expert witnesses. It is why your testimony is uniquely credible. Because you *know*. Because you have *seen* the future, and you *know* it doesn't work. Which is why whoever said the final struggle will be between the communists and the ex-communists, was right.

MARTIN *looks at* TRELAWNEY.

But I must be frank with you. If the only lesson you have learnt in all those years is that men need liberating *from* the state instead of *by* it, then your usefulness to us, to me, is pretty limited. But a defector who would stand up publicly and argue not for the roll-back of the state but for the reassertion of its full authority . . . Well, there's a man whose testimony would be listened to.

MARTIN *a slight laugh.*

But, of course, I understand, old loyalties . . .

MARTIN. That wasn't what I said.

TRELAWNEY. The sense of loyalty, old friends. That, I
completely understand.

MARTIN. Please don't. Call my commitment into question. I
know all about commitment. I once had a friend, for
instance, committed to assassinating you.

Pause.

TRELAWNEY. Exactly.

PALOCZI *comes into the downstage area.*

PALOCZI. I'm sorry, Hugh. I've lost Pavel. Has he been through
here?

TRELAWNEY. No, I don't think so.

JEREMY. In fact, we shouldn't be too long. It's snowing and of
course the bloody gritters are on strike.

TRELAWNEY. Yes, yes, of course.

PALOCZI. The latest is, apparently, the gravediggers.

TRELAWNEY. The what?

PALOCZI. Good NUPE men. It's comic, in a way. You drive
because there are no trains, you crash because the roads are
ice, and if you're killed, you lie unburied.

TRELAWNEY. Yes. My friend here thinks that basic problem in
this country is too much authority.

MARTIN (*to* JEREMY). Do you agree with this?

JEREMY. With what?

MARTIN. With what this man's been saying?

JEREMY. Why, don't you?

Pause.

MARTIN. I merely ask, for information.

JEREMY. Martin, of course, it was the state that bred it.

MARTIN. What?

JEREMY. The idea that every appetite is an entitlement.
Society an open mouth, the state a ladle.

But you know, it strikes me, something else has happened,
happened in the sixties, what you liberteenies actually did,
despite your efforts to the contrary, was not to abolish the
free market, but to take it over. Win it for your side.

Pause.

MARTIN. Go on.

JEREMY. 'Do your own thing.' 'If it feels good, fondle it.' And
if it doesn't, fondle something else.

MARTIN. Well, I can live with that.

JEREMY. Or someone else's.

And, of course, permissiveness implies permission, and
even licence must be licensed, by somebody or another. But
what has changed now is that it's the market sells the slop
that's poisoning us all and commerce that's provided the long
spoon.

A video-machine in every Porsche. A Magimix in every
microwave. And, yes, a pick-up in every lavatory. A fix in
every vein. The Prostitution Ethic. Mine, mine, mine.

Well, I don't call that liberalism, though some might, nor
socialism, though it's socialism's mutant child. I'd call it
nihilism, and unless it's understood that our disease is not
too little freedom but too much, it will destroy us all.

Pause.

TRELAWNEY. Hear hear.

Pause.

MARTIN. I see.

Pause. LERMONTOV *has come in, unnoticed by the*
OTHERS.

MARTIN. 'I'm with the malcontents, I haven't changed'?

JEREMY. Well, that does depend a bit, of course, on which
malcontents you mean.

MARTIN. There's no 'of course' about it, Jeremy.

JEREMY. Then just one question, Martin. How do you think they will react? The people who've been breastfed on the milk of social kindness all these years? When the teat is pulled away? When the plateglass is put up between them and the goodies they've been promised as of right?

I listen to the future and I'm hearing broken glass. I look into my crystal ball, and I see London burning.

With a gesture towards TRELAWNEY:

And the falcon, plotting to assassinate the falconer.

MARTIN. Now, come on, Jeremy —

PALOCZI. You know, it's very strange, to come here, from a country which has never had political or economic freedom, in the sense we understand it. It is very strange, initially, to discover that a country which has both of these good things seems to care so little about losing them. Until you realise the paradox that unless it is built on the foundations of what one might call the ultimate realities, then all freedom actually consists of is the absence of restraint. An empty canvas on which anyone may scrawl whatever vile graffiti they desire.

MARTIN. What 'ultimate realities'?

LERMONTOV. I have been looking at the pictures in your dining-hall.

The others turn to him.

Quite remarkable. So many faces, of so many dead.

It must be, I have always thought, that the condemned are blindfolded, not for themselves, but for the executioner. So he can't see their faces.

Pause.

TRELAWNEY. Was it Chesterton who said, we are fleeing from the faces of our ancestors, because that is what they are.

Long pause.

MARTIN. Look.

Slight pause.

Look, the point is, that I didn't mean . . .

As the lights fade, and the set begins to change, a picket-line crosses the stage, shouting slogans:

PICKETS (*variously*).
What do we want? Revolution!
Where do we want it? Salvador.
When do we want it? Now!
Hands off Cuba, Hands off Cuba!
Smash Pin-Pinochet! Smash Pin-Pinochet!

WEINER *crosses the stage towards the set that is beginning to build behind the picket.*

CIA — out! CIA — out! CIA — out!
Sandinistas — in! Sandinistas — in! Sandinistas — in!
The People — United — Will Never Be Defeated.
The People — United — Will Never Be Defeated.
El Pueblo — Unido — Nunca Será Vencido!
El Pueblo — Unido — Nunca Será Vencido!

And by now, WEINER *has arrived, and the* PICKET *runs out.*

Scene Five

A reception room adjacent to a banqueting hall in a large and expensive London hotel. Drinks and a telephone on a small table. A large, dark, early seventeenth century painting on the wall. There are two exits: one, left, into the banqueting hall, and the other, right, leading to the rest of the hotel.

TEDDY WEINER stands, alone. He has a drink in his hand. Like all the men in this scene, he wears a dinner jacket.

TRELAWNEY enters, quickly, right.

TRELAWNEY. Professor Weiner. Hugh Trelawney.

WEINER (*looks at his watch*). Well, hallo.

TRELAWNEY. Look, I'm so sorry, we've completely lost — Do you have a drink?

WEINER. I helped myself.

TRELAWNEY. Well done.

Pause.

Um — presumably you managed to evade the welcoming committee?

WEINER. What? Oh, sure. A quick chorus of 'Smash Pinochet' and 'Hands off Nicaragua' and I was through. I think your British picket-lines are wonderful.

TRELAWNEY. Yes.

He gets it.

Oh, yes.

A noise in the corridor.

Aha.

He turns to the right entrance as PALOCZI *and* LERMONTOV *come through it.* LERMONTOV *is in a strange, distant mood.*

PALOCZI. Hugh, Pavel was at Bush House, it over-ran two hours, I had to pick him up and change him in the cab —

WEINER (*To* LERMONTOV). Hallo, I'm Teddy Weiner. It's a privilege.

LERMONTOV *and* WEINER *shake hands.* TRELAWNEY *hands out sherry.*

LERMONTOV. We had our main problems with the tie.

PALOCZI. I know, I should have got you one of those elasticated jobs.

TRELAWNEY. Heaven forfend. A terrible American invention. Outdone, in my view, only by the verb 'eventuate'.

He realises his faux pax. WEINER *smiles.*

WEINER. As they say, America, the only country in the world to pass from barbarism to decadence without an intervening period of civilisation.

TRELAWNEY *and* PALOCZI *laugh.*

PALOCZI. Whereas, of course, where Pavel and I come from,

it's precisely opposite.

TRELAWNEY *and* WEINER *laugh*.

LERMONTOV. I did an interview today, with the BBC Russian
Service. The interviewer was a man called Griboyedov. Very
strange. He seemed to think we fought on the wrong side in
the war.

Slight pause.

TRELAWNEY. Who's we?

LERMONTOV. You are.

Slight pause.

PALOCZI. He said nothing of the kind, Pavel. He wasn't talking
about Germany.

LERMONTOV. He was talking about fascists.

PALOCZI. He was talking about Chile and Brazil.

LERMONTOV. And they're not fascists?

PALOCZI. Ask Professor Weiner. He has written quite
extensively on that very subject.

LERMONTOV *turns to* WEINER.

LERMONTOV. Well, then. Perhaps he will explain.

WEINER *a quizzical look to* TRELAWNEY, *who makes no
reaction.*

WEINER. Well, I've been known to advance the view that the
West cannot afford to be too, well, fastidious about its
choice of friends.

Slight pause.

LERMONTOV. Go on.

WEINER. If we are not to end up living in a country like your
country, Mr Lermontov.

LERMONTOV. I see.

Slight pause.

Yes, yes, I see, that's very clear. I'm sorry. You will

understand, it is a whole new — (*To* PALOCZI). Parlance, idiom?

PALOCZI. Vocabulary?

LERMONTOV. Yes.

TRELAWNEY. Well, now, perhaps —

LERMONTOV (*draining his sherry*). Indeed.

The phone rings. TRELAWNEY *picks it up.*

TRELAWNEY. Hallo?

He puts his hand over the receiver.

There's somebody in the lobby, 'needs' to speak to Mr Lermontov.

PALOCZI *takes the phone.*

PALOCZI. Hallo, now what is this?
   No, I'm not Lermontov, Mr Lermontov is about to go into dinner.
   No, I'm sorry, but he cannot possibly —
   Can't you hear what I'm saying? Do I have to spell it out in semaphore?

After a moment, he slams the phone down.

People so slow and *stupid* in this country.

LERMONTOV *goes to the phone, picks it up and dials.*

LERMONTOV. Hallo, front desk? This is P.M. Lermontov. I would like the person who has come to see me sent up, please. (*To* TRELAWNEY). Where are we now?

TRELAWNEY. The Jacobean Suite. Um, I . . .

LERMONTOV (*down the phone*). The Jacobean Suite. Thank you.

He puts the phone down.

You will understand, in the Soviet Union people spend much time, waiting in lobbies to see influential men.

Slight pause.

Please, start without me. I will miss the soup.

TRELAWNEY and WEINER look at each other. An unspoken agreement. They go out by the left door.

PALOCZI. Pavel —

LERMONTOV (*suddenly angry*). Do I have to spell it out in semaphore? Please, go away.

Pause. PALOCZI takes out a pile of postcards, on which LERMONTOV's speech is written.

PALOCZI. We didn't have enough time in the taxi. You should look through this.

He hands the cards to LERMONTOV and goes. LERMONTOV gets another drink. He starts to look through the cards. His bow-tie is uncomfortable. He fiddles with it, it comes apart. A knock, right.

LERMONTOV. Come in.

LERMONTOV shrugs, pulls the tie off, undoes the top button of his shirt, pockets the cards. He turns to see a Russian WOMAN, in her mid-forties, who has entered.

Good evening, I am Lermontov.

WOMAN. I know.

LERMONTOV. So, who are you?

WOMAN. I'm sorry to disturb you. It was in the paper, you were here tonight.

LERMONTOV. I've only got a moment, I'm afraid . . .

WOMAN. My name is Kaminskaya.

Pause.

LERMONTOV. What?

WOMAN. I work for TASS in London. Formerly a correspondent of *Izvestia*.

Pause.

And formerly to that, attached to the Military Intelligence Division of the Soviet Army. As — as a stenographer.

Pause.

Clara Ivanovna.

LERMONTOV. Oh, no.

CLARA. Do you remember?

LERMONTOV. You're in *London?*

CLARA. Yes. I wanted a new job. That work I was doing on *Izvestia.* There's only so long, you can do that stuff. I imagine it's the same here, writing the letters to the *Daily Mail.*

LERMONTOV. I don't believe this.

CLARA. How do you find it? I find the most striking thing is the trivia. Not the pornography, just the torrential triviality, each way you turn.

LERMONTOV. I just do not believe this.

CLARA. And the lack of books in people's houses. Working-class people. You would think, at least a set of Dickens, Rudyard Kipling —

LERMONTOV. This is — *preposterous.* The man is — *in there.*

CLARA. Who's in there?

LERMONTOV. The boy who I released, in Budapest. Who threw the hand-grenade.

CLARA. What hand-grenade?

Pause. LERMONTOV *looks at* CLARA.

LERMONTOV. I am aware that there are rules. Grades of invective. 'Childish, scurrilous and egotistical' for signing a petition, 'hoarse, malicious and unsavoury' for an interview with Western correspondents, 'slanderous, corrupt and cynically treacherous' for a pamphlet published in the West. But what was visited on me broke all the rules. That wasn't from some well-thumbed manual. That wasn't faceless. It was sharp and real, and *personal.*

CLARA. Yes. It was personal.

LERMONTOV. Then — *why?*

CLARA. Because —

LERMONTOV. Why did you come here?

CLARA. Because you were coming here. Because you have been seduced into the camp of the most bellicose cold war imperialists. And I did want to know —

LERMONTOV. 'The camp of the most bellicose —'

CLARA. Yes, the language is a little arch. A little coarse and breathless. It's the vocabulary, in fact, of people who until quite recently were stupid peasants, working with wooden ploughs. Until they were all sent off to school, and taught at least a kind of language.

LERMONTOV. At what a cost.

CLARA. One of the great achievements, you may think, of the Great October Revolution. A victory comparable with that of the Red Army in the Civil War.

LERMONTOV. Oh, please —

CLARA. Or indeed the five year plan. Those thousands upon thousands of young party cadres, laying pipelines across Russia's freezing wastes.

LERMONTOV. These words —

CLARA. Those superhuman tasks. Against all odds. At any cost.

LERMONTOV. I have, I have read the picture books. I do, I know these words —

CLARA. You see, it just isn't true, that the only way that people will do anything is if they're bribed or forced at the point of a revolver. There are times, Pavel Mikhailovich, when it just isn't true.

LERMONTOV *looks at* CLARA.

It's just, at other times . . . Most times . . .
    People get tired. They can't go on. Suddenly, the odds seem stacked too heavily against them, and the cost appears too great. Even the most heroic superman flops down onto the ground, and realises that he's just a normal human being after all.

And turns his tired eyes to people who will tell him what to do. And sullenly, resentfully, submissively, does what he's told.

Returns to normal life.

Pause.

LERMONTOV. So?

CLARA. So, you don't pretend it never happened.

LERMONTOV. This is just absurd.

CLARA. What is absurd?

LERMONTOV. I am standing in a suite in a hotel in London, being lectured by a woman who put me in a labour camp.

CLARA. Well, now I have a face.

LERMONTOV. You knew *I* had a face.

CLARA. You're right. I'd seen it.

LERMONTOV. But you still —

CLARA. I'd seen it sneering in contempt, at a stupid girl from a Russian village, who knew nothing about music, who had never seen a city and who didn't always understand when people shouted at her very loud.

Pause.

LERMONTOV. I see.

Pause.

Eight years.

Pause.

I see.

TRELAWNEY *and* PALOCZI *enter.*

Well, there he is. The boy who I released. Who was exactly who we thought he was. To whom I gave a hand-grenade.

CLARA *looks at* PALOCZI, *then quickly to* LERMONTOV *and then goes out quickly.*

PALOCZI. Pavel, who was that woman?

LERMONTOV. You don't know?

PALOCZI. Please what is going on, Pavel?

LERMONTOV. I might ask you, the same question. I might ask you, what has happened to the brave young revolutionary, full of dreams, who understood why peasants brought free food to feed the cities, and who clearly doesn't understand that any more.

PALOCZI. Please, what is this about?

LERMONTOV. And who will tell us — *now* — what he thinks that *that* was all about?

Pause.

PALOCZI. It isn't very difficult. It's very simple. For a man who came here from a country which has not possessed a real border for a thousand years. Quite simple. God save Hungary.

Pause.

LERMONTOV. That wasn't what you said.

PALOCZI. It wasn't what I thought. But it was what I felt.

MARTIN *enters quickly.*

MARTIN. I'm sorry. Look, am I very late?

LERMONTOV. I would like to know, I would like to be informed. Exactly what is happening here today.

TRELAWNEY (*with a glance at* PALOCZI). I'm so sorry. Didn't anyone explain?

Slight pause.

The Committee in Defence of Liberty, is a body dedicated to the simple notion that we face two enemies, in Britain, one without and one within. Without, we face a rapacious military power, bent on conquest and subordination; while within, we see a society so soft, so feeble and degenerate that we fear it may have lost, quite literally, its will to live.

And despite the fashionable nostra of the day, we do suspect that the economics of the corner grocer's shop, while

admirable values in themselves, may not prove quite
sufficient as a means to reassert the basic, fundamental
instincts of the nation.

And so — resistance to aggression from without; the
reassertion of authority within. You are speaking to the next
Government of Britain, Mr Lermontov. Which is why we are
so keen to hear what you have got to say.

Pause. LERMONTOV *reaches in his pocket, takes out the
pile of cards which* PALOCZI *gave him. He glances at them.
He realises he still holds his black tie in his hand.*

LERMONTOV. Could someone help me, please?

Scene Six

*The top table of a banquet. Flowers bedeck, white linen gleams.
Behind the table sit — from left to right — JEREMY,
TRELAWNEY, WEINER, LERMONTOV, PALOCZI, MARTIN.
A statuette in front of* WEINER. TRELAWNEY *stands, and
speaks into the microphone.*

TRELAWNEY. Professor Weiner. (*He sits.*)

WEINER (*stands*). Gentlemen, I hope you will forgive me, if I
address what I have to say, on your behalf, directly to Pavel
Mikhailovich. Because I feel that what ought to be said must
take the form of an apology, an apology which must be made
by us, the West, to those brave men who have stood up for
their beliefs in Budapest, in Prague, in Warsaw and indeed in
Moscow, whom I think we have betrayed.

And I don't mean just by lack of military support, though
that's important, but by a kind of lie that we've been living,
about what we are and what we have become. Most of all, a
lie about those people out there in the street, who are as we
well know the same ones who ten years ago were marching
for the US to get out of Vietnam, and for Black Power, peace
and love and indeed the whole shebang. And in your
presence it behooves us — those of us who argued for so long
that those folks were at least idealists, at least sincere — to
put ourselves in the witness box, to test that testimony, to

tell it how it really is.

Pause. A little cough. Then:

To affirm that agitation's agitation, even if it's published quarterly in learned periodicals, and that subversion is subversion, even if the subverters of our culture are distinguished film directors, poets, writers and musicians. And that treachery is treachery, even if the traitors to our country have no need of telephoto lenses, tape-machines and microfilm, but ply their trade as smart left lawyers, clever linguists, and conscience-striken academics.

And, for I think these matters are connected, that mobs of hooligans are mobs of hooligans, even if they happen to consist of college students, teachers and professors. And that parasites are parasites, whether they are feeding off the state as clients, or as members of that army of administrators who, with such precious, finely-honed compassion, dole out our largesse.

PALOCZI *has been looking at a particular card in the pile. He removes it from the pile. He writes another card.*

And even worse than that, to admit that it's our fault. To confess that in order to assuage our overwhelming sense of guilt, we spawned a generation so soft and so effete, so resistant to responsibility of any kind, that it is not prepared to die, or even really live, for anything beyond its own sense of material and moral satisfaction. And, worst of all, that we snatched away from them at birth the only antidote there is to the sickly and corrosive culture of appeasement and surrender they've created. I mean, a sense of who they really are. I mean those gut emotions, instincts, prejudices even, that are in fact the only things that men have ever really found worth living or worth dying for. I mean . . .

I mean that it has taken me some time: it has taken me the best part of a lifetime, to admit, without embarrassment or hesitation: that I belong to the nation of my birth.

Pause.

And if I may say so, Pavel Mikhailovich, it has taken you and people like you, voices issuing from the darkness of a nationhood suppressed, to convince me of that fact.

Pause.

And so — please accept our welcome, and our admiration, and our thanks.

Applause, as WEINER *hands the statuette to* LERMONTOV. LERMONTOV *stands to receive it. As* WEINER *sits and passes the microphone,* PALOCZI *hands* LERMONTOV *the cards.* LERMONTOV *coughs and begins to speak.*

LERMONTOV. Thank you. May I say first of all how good it is to spend an evening discussing freedom. Particularly as, in my country, no one is free to hold such a discussion. May I also thank the organisers for providing such a — (*To* PALOCZI.) What's this?

PALOCZI. Sumptuous.

LERMONTOV. Sumptuous — repast; and Professor Weiner for such a generous and indeed inspiring speech. I think the phrase is, 'follow that'.

He turns to a new card written by PALOCZI *during* WEINER's *speech. As he does so, an ad lib:*

Well, I will do my best.

I was particularly struck by his remarks on the surrender of the West and those people who have made a career of promoting this surrender. I would — morely?

PALOCZI. Merely.

LERMONTOV. Merely remark in passing, to those who would be rather red than dead, that there are many graves where I have recently come from, which confirm that they may not have the option.

Turns cards. Back on the pre-written text.

And I must thank those gentlemen who selected me as a recipient of this award. I am most honoured. But I must say that I do not view this award as mine alone. I view it as being for all the zeks, in all the camps, the living and the dead.

New card.

For the seventies and the one-nine-oh-threes, the one-nine-oh-ones and the two-oh-nines, the two-sixties and the sixty-fours, the violators, great and small, of the Criminal Code of the Russian Federated Socialist Republic.

He turns the card. The next card is not the one he expects. He realises that PALOCZI *has removed it. He sees it on the table. He picks it up quickly and reads:*

From the agitators and subversives, violators of the public order, slanderers and hooligans and parasites and traitors, of the Soviet Corrective Labour Colonies.

Pause.

Who up until their sentences were teachers, physicists, academicians and administrators. Writers and poets. Actors, film directors and musicians. Workers and trade union officials. Linguists and lawyers. Publishers. Professors.

Pause.

People who, resist.

A very long pause, as LERMONTOV *looks through the rest of the cards. Then he looks up.*

I appear — to be expected — to advance the view — that the bombing of my country, and of yours — is preferable to the greater evil — of, surrender.

Pause. He places the cards on the table.

It is not of course the same. It is not —

To PALOCZI:

— equivalent, to be compared with?

Pause.

PALOCZI. Comparable.

LERMONTOV. Comparable. Of course. You have no camps. Your 'dissidents' are free. It is no way comparable.
  And yet.
  I wonder, can there be anything as bad as telling someone that they only think the things they think because they're

'cranks' or 'crazies'? How, um —

To PALOCZI:

Caustic, eaten into, rust, decay?

PALOCZI. I don't know —

LERMONTOV (*with a gesture to* WEINER). Yes, *corrosive,* of
a human being's dignity?

Pause.

I'm sorry. I have not fulfilled my duty. Pavel Mikhailovich
has not reminded you of what he was supposed to. He has
not affirmed 'the ultimate realities'. But he will nonetheless
say something. It is this.

He breathes deeply. Then:

That if you really want to see a nation, strong and tough and
virile, marching to a single rhythm, banged out with a
hammer on a rail, then — please, gentlemen — come to my
country.

It is not that it's the same.

It's just — that it does appear to be — the same variety of
people — who applaud it on their own side — but oppose it
on the other. People for whom, the ultimate reality is not in
fact resistance, but —

To PALOCZI, *as it were in Russian:*

Control, administration? People in control?

PALOCZI. I'm sorry?

LERMONTOV. You know. Police, the army, running things?

PALOCZI. What do you mean, Pavel?

LERMONTOV (*gesturing at* TRELAWNEY). He used the word.
I heard him use the word.

PALOCZI. Pavel, you are behaving like a child!

LERMONTOV *remembers. In 'English'.*

LERMONTOV. 'Authority'.

He turns out front. Back in 'English':

I'm sorry. Slight problem of translation. Yes.

You see, I look around this room, and I don't see faces which have ever seen the world through wire. Yours are not gaolers' faces. But perhaps they are the faces of the people who employ the gaolers.

Faces which cannot remember, if they ever knew, the superhuman things that people can achieve, when for a moment they forget what they've been told they are.

Pause.

I'm sorry. How embarrassing of me.

He picks up the statuette.

And I am most honoured. Most —

He can't find the synonym. A glance to PALOCZI. *He changes his mind.*

Most honoured.

But I have decided. No.

He puts down the statuette.

You will I hope forgive me.

LERMONTOV *goes. Long pause.* PALOCZI *stands, abruptly, and goes out too. Pause.* TRELAWNEY *looks at his watch. Then, almost as if he'd just remembered some pressing engagement, he stands and goes.* WEINER, *rather efficiently, as if it was the end of the event, tidies his napkin, pockets his notes, and goes.* MARTIN *stands.* JEREMY *stands.* MARTIN *and* JEREMY *alone.*

JEREMY. Martin, he's wrong. Just because he's suffered, just because he's brave, a hero, doesn't mean he can't be wrong.

MARTIN. I stood there for an hour. Stood across the street. Those faces. Couldn't move.

Outburst:

I mean, come on, Jeremy, with hand on heart, do you really want a man like that to run the country?

JEREMY. Who?

MARTIN. Trelawney?

JEREMY. Yes.

MARTIN. We sack the nanny, hire a governess? Her motto, heed the mystic voices of our ancestors?

JEREMY. Well, that's certainly one way of —

MARTIN. So, then, what do you predict, for Hugh Trelawney's brave new world? The rope? The cat? The censor? Military conscription?

JEREMY. Well, I wouldn't be at all —

MARTIN. 'In the end the only way to make men uniform is to put them all in one?'

JEREMY. Martin. What follows, surely, even you can understand. That man is like he is because those people in the street are like you were. Because what he says has got to happen is indeed the only way to win the war.

MARTIN. 'Objectively'?

JEREMY. Correct. In the same way that —

MARTIN. Why does this matter quite so much to you?

JEREMY. Because you're right.

MARTIN. Well, glory be.

JEREMY. In a way, yes, I do wish I'd been a Red at Trinity. Wish that instead of having to betray my class, I could have, merely, come in from the cold.

  And if *I* can sacrifice that whey-faced child who thought the toiling masses were about to rise and forget the New Jerusalem, then why the hell can't you?

Pause. He changes tone.

You see, you come to realise, it really is the little things. The sensual things. The smell of woodsmoke. Mulled wine, warming chilly fingers. The family's Wellingtons, all lined up in the hall. But that come the crunch, you'll take up arms, you'll maim and kill, to keep those things. The past that you rejected, but I never had, you see.

Pause.

MARTIN. What should I do?

    Pause.

JEREMY. Take the last step, Martin. And Go Home.

    TRELAWNEY *stands there.*

TRELAWNEY. They've gone.

JEREMY. Who've gone?

TRELAWNEY. The Barbarians Without The Gates.

    Pause.

JEREMY. Is it not Leon Trotsky who reminds us, there is such a thing as human dust.

    TRELAWNEY *goes out. Behind him stands a child in her early teens, wearing a portable stereo. She wears a CND badge. It is* TANIA, AMANDA's *daughter. Darkness on* MARTIN *and* JEREMY.

Scene Seven

Summer. The early 1980s.

    Green hangings, representing trees and foliage. TANIA *sings along with the song she's hearing on her stereo.*

    Upstage, a YOUNG MAN *cycles on. He wears a slouch hat and a long mackintosh. He looks a bit like a gangster.*

    The YOUNG MAN *comes to a halt, gets off his bike, and leans against it, waiting for something or somebody.*

    TANIA *turns and goes out as a second* CYCLIST *enters, a slightly seedy, middle-aged man. It is* PUGACHEV. *The first cyclist calls out to him. It is* KOROLENKO.

KOROLENKO. Well. Comrade Pugachev.

    PUGACHEV *comes to a quick halt.*

PUGACHEV. Uh — yes?

KOROLENKO. What a pleasant chance to meet here, in the park. How are you?

    PUGACHEV *dismounts and lays his bicycle on the ground.*

PUGACHEV (*bemused*). Oh, I'm — very well.

KOROLENKO (*no change of tone, still light and conversational*). I've been looking for you a whole week. My pass ran out four days ago. I'm Anatoly Korolenko.

PUGACHEV (*taking out a cigarette*). Pardon?

KOROLENKO (*lighting PUGACHEV's cigarette*). I'm a friend of Lermontov. Your friend.

PUGACHEV *drops his voice.*

PUGACHEV. What do you want?

KOROLENKO (*drops his voice*). I'm told you travel. Other countries.

PUGACHEV. Sometimes.

KOROLENKO (*light and conversational again*). I'm a miner. I was exiled to Vorkuta in the Northern Urals. They introduced new schedules in the pits. The workers told them they were crazy. Big explosion. Fifty died.

PUGACHEV (*low voice*). What has this to do with me?

KOROLENKO. There's this little group. In Leningrad. Donetsk. some other places. We're a kind of unofficial union. We've got this manifesto. We want to get it out.

PUGACHEV (*low voice*). I don't travel to the West. Well, not that often. Mainly the DDR, and Hungary and Poland. Places like that.

KOROLENKO. Exactly.

Pause.

Will you take it, then? The manifesto?

PUGACHEV. No, of course I won't.

KOROLENKO. It's titled 'For our freedom — and for yours'.

Pause.

PUGACHEV. Look. I'm a Professor at the University of Moscow. I'm not that good at thinking on my feet.

He looks round, warily.

Particularly, in the middle of the day.

KOROLENKO mounts his bike. Briskly:

KOROLENKO. Right, then. At nightfall. We will meet.

Looks at PUGACHEV.

And then you'll tell me.

AMANDA (*off*). Tania! Tanny, where are you?

Lights fade on PUGACHEV and KOROLENKO. A wire fence falls between them and the entering AMANDA. Lights only downstage now. MARTIN follows AMANDA on to the stage.

Tanny!

She turns back to MARTIN.

They're some of them so frighteningly young.

MARTIN. Indeed.

AMANDA. But very brave.

MARTIN. That doesn't mean they're right.

Two WOMEN, one of them in her 40s, enter from stage left. The older WOMAN has a map. They look around and go out right.

Well, obviously not *all* —

AMANDA. Oh, no. In fact, I was surprised, how various —

MARTIN. And you are seriously considering, yourself —

AMANDA. I've not made up my mind.

Slight pause.

It was Tanny, really. She was desperate to come.

TANIA has entered.

MARTIN. And here she is, by all that's wonderful?

AMANDA. She is indeed. Hey, Tan —

TANIA is wearing headphones, so can't hear.

Hey, Tanny —

TANIA *spots* AMANDA's *wave and takes off her headphones.*

D'you remember Martin?

Pause.

TANIA. Oh, yuh. 'Course.

With a grin.

'That fucking renegade.'

Slight pause.

AMANDA. Yes. That's the one.

The two WOMEN *enter from right.*

1ST WOMAN. There's a kind of copse. It's sheltered by the trees. We'll set up there.

They go out left.

TANIA. Well, still . . . It's only rock and roll.

She grins, turns, and follows the two WOMEN *out.* AMANDA *breathes deeply.*

MARTIN. You know, there's this little, stained-glass St Anne, in the Lady Chapel of our church, the spit —

AMANDA. You go to church?

MARTIN. I'm the anchor of the baritones.

Slight pause.

We only get a service every other week, but the padre is a sound, no nonsense chap. Soup only to the conspicuously needy. Lucky, because in Lower Purley they've this bloke who appears to think Pol Pot was basically sound, just a little soft on the urban middle class.

So what's your present bag, then? Apart, that is, from Battered Lesbians Against the Bomb?

Pause.

AMANDA. I'm running a resources centre.

MARTIN. Well well well. I run a XJ12.

Pause.

AMANDA. There's gold in them thar Tory think-tanks, then?

MARTIN. Well, silver, certainly. What in God's name —

AMANDA. Well, I say 'run'. It's more of a collective.

MARTIN. Naturally.

AMANDA. We produce a kind of newspaper. Do have a copy.

MARTIN (*taking a copy*). Thanks.

> *The* TWO WOMEN, *a* 3RD WOMAN, *and* TANIA *cross the stage, carrying camping equipment. They go out right.*

> Well, this is all quite clear. 'Facilities.' 'Advice bureaux.' The Women's Movement. Peace Groups. 'Black Defence Campaigns.' From whom does who wish to 'reclaim the night?' What in the name of all that's holy is 'alternative technology?'

> *The* 2ND WOMAN *crosses the stage from right to left.*

AMANDA. Oh, you know, finding ways of making things that people actually need. Like, ploughshares, as opposed to swords.

MARTIN. I see.

AMANDA. Oh, Martin, what the fuck's gone wrong with you?

> *The* 2ND WOMAN *has re-entered left, dragging a huge sheet of polythene. The* 1ST *and* 3RD WOMEN, *and* TANIA *have come in stage right to help her.*

2ND WOMAN. They've closed the south gate. And they're clearing space around the hangers. That usually means there's an alert.

MARTIN. That always means there's an alert.

1ST WOMAN. Oh, yur? How do you know?

MARTIN. I live here. You are dragging polythene across my property.

Pause.

3RD WOMAN. Who is this creep?

TANIA. Oh, it's this bloke who used —

AMANDA. He's what he says he is. He lives there, in that house. It used to be his father's house. And he's just bought it back.

1ST WOMAN. I thought he was a friend of yours.

AMANDA. He was. Now he's the person who could call the police and have you all removed.

MARTIN. Now can I ask, of whoever is in charge here —

2ND WOMAN. Look. The land was common. The land between 'your land' and the perimeter of the US Air Force property. Last week, the Council repossessed the land, and sold it to the base. So, yesterday, at dawn, we were ejected, *that* was built, and hence, today —

MARTIN. I have fairies at the bottom of my garden.

Pause.

I was thinking more in terms of an injunction.

3RD WOMAN. Wouldn't work.

MARTIN. You wanna bet?

1ST WOMAN. Injunctions require names. We have no names.

MARTIN. Is this a metaphysical —

3RD WOMAN. Or put another way, you find our names and the court may order us to go. And go we will. But others will take over. And the same thing will keep happening.

Slight pause.

We — in the sense of this — we have no names.

1ST WOMAN. No membership.

2ND WOMAN. And no committees.

3RD WOMAN. No printing press. No postal code. No phone.

2ND WOMAN. And I assure you — nobody 'in charge'.

Pause.

MARTIN. Well, you got it all worked out.

1ST WOMAN. No, not 'it all'. Just this.

The WOMEN *go out.*

AMANDA. It doesn't actually need working out.

MARTIN. Oh, no?

AMANDA. Any more than for all my silly people with their weird and wonderful campaigns.

MARTIN. You're sure?

AMANDA. And of course you may say that the urge to stop the planet being blown to blazes is a form of brute, material self-interest —

MARTIN. Well, that's certainly an argument —

AMANDA. Or that to want these aeroplanes to be removed is merely good old British national pride —

MARTIN. Well, nobody likes Yanks —

AMANDA. But I think in fact that in the end what they are doing, what we all are trying to do, in our many different ways, can only be accounted for by something in the nature of our species which resents, rejects and ultimately will resist a world that is demonstrably and in this case dramatically wrong and mad and unjust and unfair.

And I wonder, Martin, if you ever really felt like that. Or, if you did, if you can still remember.

MARTIN. No.

Pause.

No, as it happens, I don't think I do.

Pause.

AMANDA. So. Are you going to call the police?

MARTIN. Tomorrow. Are you going to stay?

AMANDA. Tonight.

Suddenly, a LOUDSPEAKER *blares, as the lights quickly fade.*

LOUDSPEAKER. Scorcher. We have Scorcher. I repeat, we have

a Scorcher.

Sirens begin to wail. Dogs bark. Beyond the wire, searchlights and running men. Huge doors open, revealing headlamps. Engines rev.

Cresta Run. We are go for Cresta Run.

The headlamps — of trucks and motorcycles — career downstage, up to the wire. The lights beam through the wire, dazzling the audience. The lights flash. Engines revving wildly.

Kiss. We are kiss. Repeat, all units. We are kiss.

The sirens fade. The headlamps die, as the 'vehicles' reverse away.
    Silence.
    But just before it's total, two cycle headlamps, illuminating PUGACHEV *and* KOROLENKO *on their bicycles.*

KOROLENKO. Well, then?

PUGACHEV. How long.

KOROLENKO. How long?

PUGACHEV. Do you think you'll last? A week, a month, a year?

KOROLENKO. Maybe. Who knows? 'May Days.'

Maydays

5 May 1818	Karl Marx born
15 May 1848	Communist rising in Paris: quickly overthrown
28 May 1871	Paris Commune falls after 14 months in power
1 May 1886	Chicago General Strike for eight hour day leads to five executions and the founding of the international May Day workers' festival
31 May 1917	Bolsheviks achieve majority in Petrograd Soviet
4 May 1919	Bavarian Soviet defeated after two weeks in power
4 May 1926	British General Strike begins — "Nine Days in May"
3 May 1936	Popular Front Government elected in France
3 May 1937	Communists suppress anarchists in Barcelona
2 May 1945	Berlin falls to the Red Army
7 May 1954	French defeated by Communist Vietnamese at Dien Bien Phu
10 May 1968	Parisian "Night of the Barricades" sparks movements towards General Strike
4 May 1970	Four American students shot dead during anti-war demonstrations at Kent State University, Ohio
1 May 1973	Two million British workers strike against anti-union legislation
3 May 1979	Margaret Thatcher wins General Election
2 May 1982	British task force sinks the *General Belgrano*

Methuen's Modern Plays

Jean Anouilh	*Antigone*
	Becket
	The Lark
John Arden	*Serjeant Musgrave's Dance*
	The Workhouse Donkey
	Armstrong's Last Goodnight
John Arden and	*The Business of Good Government*
Margaretta D'Arcy	*The Royal Pardon*
	The Hero Rises Up
	The Island of the Mighty
	Vandaleur's Folly
Wolfgang Bauer	*Shakespeare the Sadist*
Rainer Werner	
Fassbinder	*Bremen Coffee*
Peter Handke	*My Foot My Tutor*
Frank Xaver Kroetz	*Stallerhof*
Brendan Behan	*The Quare Fellow*
	The Hostage
	Richard's Cork Leg
Edward Bond	*A-A-America!* and *Stone*
	Saved
	Narrow Road to the Deep North
	The Pope's Wedding
	Lear
	The Sea
	Bingo
	The Fool and *We Come to the River*
	Theatre Poems and Songs
	The Bundle
	The Woman
	The Worlds with *The Activists Papers*
	Restoration and *The Cat*
	Summer and *Fables*
Bertolt Brecht	*Mother Courage and Her Children*
	The Caucasian Chalk Circle
	The Good Person of Szechwan
	The Life of Galileo

	The Threepenny Opera
	Saint Joan of the Stockyards
	The Resistible Rise of Arturo Ui
	The Mother
	Mr Puntila and His Man Matti
	The Measures Taken and other Lebrstücke
	The Days of the Commune
	The Messingkauf Dialogues
	Man Equals Man and *The Elephant Calf*
	The Rise and Fall of the City of Mahagonny and *The Seven Deadly sins*
	Baal
	A Respectable Wedding and other one-act plays
	Drums in the Night
	In the Jungle of Cities
	Fear and Misery of the Third Reich and *Senora Carrar's Rifles*
Brecht ⎫ Weill ⎬ Lane ⎭	*Happy End*
Howard Brenton	*The Churchill Play*
	Weapons of Happiness
	Epsom Downs
	The Romans in Britain
	Plays for the Poor Theatre
	Magnificence
	Revenge
	Hitler Dances
Howard Brenton and David Hare	*Brassneck*
Mikhail Bulgakov	*The White Guard*
Noël Coward	*Hay Fever*
Shelagh Delaney	*A Taste of Honey*
	The Lion in Love
David Edgar	*Destiny*
	Mary Barnes

	The Monster of Karlovy Vary and *Then and Now*
	No Limits To Love
Arthur Miller	*The American Clock*
Percy Mtwa, Mbongeni Ngema, Barney Simon	*Woza Albert*
Peter Nichols	*Passion Play*
	Poppy
Joe Orton	*Loot*
	What the Butler Saw
	Funeral Games and *The Good and Faithful Servant*
	Entertaining Mr Sloane
	Up Against It
Harold Pinter	*The Birthday Party*
	The Room and *The Dumb Waiter*
	The Caretaker
	A Slight Ache and other plays
	The Collection and *The Lover*
	The Homecoming
	Tea Party and other plays
	Landscape and *Silence*
	Old Times
	No Man's Land
	Betrayal
	The Hothouse
	Other Places (A Kind of Alaska, Victoria Station, Family Voices)
Luigi Pirandello	*Henry IV*
	Six Characters in Search of an Author
Stephen Poliakoff	*Hitting Town* and *City Sugar*
David Rudkin	*The Sons of Light*
	The Triumph of Death
Jean-Paul Sartre	*Crime Passionnel*
Wole Soyinka	*Madmen and Specialists*
	The Jero Plays
	Death and the King's Horseman
	A Play of Giants

C.P. Taylor   *And a Nightingale Sang . . .*
                       Good
Peter Whelan   *The Accrington Pals*
Nigel Williams   *Line 'Em*
                       Class Enemy
Charles Wood   *Veterans*
Theatre Workshop   *Oh What a Lovely War!*
Various authors   *Best Radio Plays of 1978* (Don
                           Haworth: *Episode on a Thursday
                           Evening:* Tom Mallin: *Halt! Who
                           Goes There?;* Jennifer Phillips:
                           Daughters of Men; Fay Weldon:
                           Polaris; Jill Hyem: *Remember Me;*
                           Richard Harris: *Is It Something I
                           Said?*)
                       Best Radio Plays of 1979 (Shirley Gee:
                           Typhoid Mary; Carey Harrison: *I
                           Never Killed My German;* Barrie
                           Keeffe: *Heaven Scent;* John
                           Kirkmorris: *Coxcombe;* John
                           Peacock: *Attard in Retirement;* Olwen
                           Wymark: *The Child*)
                       Best Radio Plays of 1982 (Rhys
                           Adrian:*Watching the Plays Together;*
                           John Arden: *The Old Man Sleeps
                           Alone;* Harry Barton: *Hoopoe Day;*
                           Donald Chapman: *Invisible Writing;*
                           Tom Stoppard: *The Dog It Was
                           That Died;* William Trevor: *Autumn
                           Sunshine*)

If you would like to receive, free of charge, regular information about new plays and theatre books from Methuen, please send your name and address to:

The Marketing Department (Drama)
Methuen London Ltd
North Way
Andover
Hampshire SP10 5BE